"I LOVE ~~hate~~ negotiating"

**CHANGE YOUR THINKING
AND LEARN HOW TO
GET WHAT YOU WANT**

Sam Trattles

A CIP catalogue of this book is available from the National Library of Australia.

Trattles, Sam

I Love Negotiating

ISBN: 978-0-9944507-1-5

Cover design: Melissa Mylchreest

Sub editors: Kate Warner, Sarah Pickette

Layout: John Aquilina

I love Negotiating is available to purchase at:

www.samtrattles.com

This easy-to-use workbook will guide you through the highs and lows of the negotiation process. It will help you shift your mindset, build your confidence and approach negotiations with ease.

To my amazing, blended, loving,

individual and caring family – I am

blessed to be among this crowd. xo

Dear Princess

You know this would never have been completed without your input (2pol2 for the post print credit :) Thanks + for always making me laugh me to take advantage reminding me to take advantage of all opportunities – you never know where a great story will unfold.

Br. Silom

lots of love Amy x

Contents

about
this
book

Introduction

Many people carry around an unnecessary fear of negotiating. This fear creates resistance and ultimately hinders your success – regardless of how much you want or think you deserve something. I want to help you build your confidence, overcome that fear, and set you on the path to successful negotiating.

You may think that only certain people are good at it, that negotiating isn't for everyone. Perhaps you've even suspected that it has a touch of the dark arts about it, and that only a select few know how to do it well. "It's just not me", "I'm no good at it", "I hate negotiating!"...sound familiar?

I can assure you that negotiating is a skill that EVERYONE can be good at. There is an art to it, but it's one that YOU can learn. This book will guide you through the processes and pitfalls of negotiation to help you master this art.

Firstly, it's important to understand what's been getting in your way so far. I bet you have a good job, you're probably well-educated, highly skilled in your field, and are even known for being confident. So why is it that you feel anxious at the thought of negotiating for something you really want?

If you break into a sweat, or start thinking of ways to avoid entering into a negotiation, this book is for you!

If you expect – and fear – that the negotiation process will be uncomfortable and stressful, it will be. And it will stop you from getting what you want. NOW is the time for you to be brave, be bold and get more of what you want, with ease!

Why me?

Well, I am one of the lucky ones who just happen to love negotiating. It's true. I learnt early on that negotiating can help me get what I want. Not only that, it can be fun. Negotiating is so much a part of my life now, I don't even notice that I'm doing it. For me, it's a habit – and a good one.

I learnt to negotiate on the job – assessing, negotiating and closing commercial deals over many years in various corporate roles. I am very lucky as I had great mentors, managers and excellent commercially minded, legal-support people to learn from.

I made a LOT of mistakes and I probably upset a few people along the way by pushing too hard – through my lack of experience and understanding. If you're one of those people, please accept my apologies. I learnt so much from these mistakes, but I'm sorry you ended up being an unwitting guinea pig.

One of the simplest lessons I learnt was to understand that not everything is negotiable. Learning when to push and when to pull needs guidance and practice.

In my many years on the 'buy-side' (budget owner side) of a negotiation, I don't ever recall attending a training session focused on negotiation tactics. And I certainly didn't learn these skills at school.

Meanwhile, the many sales teams I sat next to were frequently trained in the art of chasing down and closing deals, learning new and innovative ways to get customers to part with their money.

Why is it that only the sales teams got this training? This seemed unfair to me, and was one of the reasons I wanted to write this book: to provide people who are buying something significant with a reference guide on how to negotiate more easily, particularly with those highly trained sales people.

As the budget owner for projects worth millions of dollars, it was commonly mistaken that my role in negotiations was simply to bring cash to the table. But that was not the bottom line. My primary responsibility was to ensure that we got the best deal, the most value for money and the greatest return on investment.

So, regardless of what size budget you are working with, the pressure is on to obtain maximum value from what you purchase. This was another reason I wanted to write this book: to help make sure you never get ripped off again.

Over the years I've heard the words, "I hate negotiating", thousands of times. I find it shocking (and a little sad) that the thought of negotiating turns generally confident people to jelly.

This is the final reason I decided to write this book: I want to help all the curious, confident and capable people out there who want to develop this skill, but don't know where to start.

My idea is simple: to translate what I have learnt from commercial deals into knowledge that can help you shift your mindset and empower you to get more of what you want.

I want to give you tactics and strategies that you can practice to help you turn this skill into a lifelong habit. I want you to approach it with excitement and confidence and clarity. But most of all, I want to see you enjoying the benefits of your new-found love for negotiating!

How to use this book

- To start with, I will share some information about why we don't love negotiating and help you understand why now is the time to embrace this skill.
- Next, you will learn how to identify what type of negotiator you are. Once you understand where you are on this spectrum, you can focus your efforts on working through the exercises that mostly apply to you, to help you deliver results quickly.
- Think of this book as a kind of 'Choose Your Own Adventure'; you can skip the bits that you are confident with, and instead focus on the areas that need work.
- This book is structured as a workbook, so please write in it, on it and around it. I know it feels naughty – but go on, do it!!
- I hope you hold onto this book for many years, and keep referring back to it. You will find that as you develop your skills, your confidence will also grow, enabling you to negotiate more and more complicated deals.

What to expect from this book

- As you make your way through the chapters, you will go through a series of activities to help you build your confidence.
- Each activity will give you practical tips, scripts, strategies and tools to use while practicing.
- Don't worry if you're unable to complete all of the activities straight away, the intention is that you will work your way through this book over time and, as your confidence builds, you will be able to work through the more challenging activities at each of the levels.

Outcomes from reading this book

- By the time you complete this book you will no longer fear negotiating.
- Negotiation will start to become a habit, just part of what you do, without any hesitation or anxiety.
- You will have the ability to negotiate like a master when it's required of you.
- And maybe, just maybe, you might start to love it...

Notes

_____

_____

_____

_____

_____

_____

_____

_____

_____

_____

_____

_____

_____

_____

_____

_____

_____

_____

_____

_____

_____

_____

_____

_____

about

you

About you

About you

Your initial thoughts about negotiating

Let's start with how you really feel about negotiating. This will help you understand your true feelings about it and enable you to identify what's holding you back. Once this is done, you'll know what skills you need to focus on developing.

Your self awareness map

Write down any thoughts and feelings that come to mind when you think of negotiating.

- How have you felt in the past when you've had to negotiate a situation at work or with your family, etc?
- What words or phrases spring to mind (positive or negative) when you think about buying something of significance, etc?

Write these in the thought bubbles on the next page; try and fill up each of them with a word or sentence.

Notes

_____

_____

_____

_____

_____

_____

_____

_____

_____

_____

_____

_____

_____

_____

_____

_____

_____

_____

_____

_____

_____

My self awareness map

Let's drill down

Digging a little deeper now into how you think about negotiations, it's time to be more specific. For each of the following questions, rate how you feel about them (using either the faces or numbers scale).

Overall attitude

How do you feel, generally, about negotiating?

0   2   4   6   8   10

Current state

How good a negotiator do you think you are now?

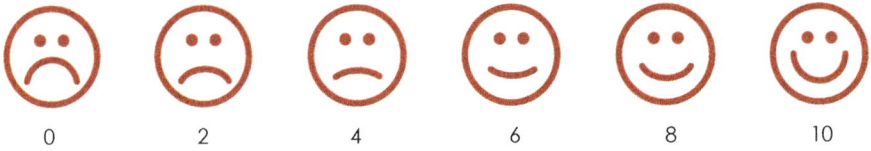

0   2   4   6   8   10

Future state

How good a negotiator would you like to be?

0   2   4   6   8   10

If your 'state' has moved up the scale, then keep reading – this book is for you! Most people who are confident in other parts of their life, but have challenges with negotiating, want to get better at this skill. Reading this book will set you on the path to demystifying (and mastering) the art of negotiating.

What's holding you back?

Now it's time to consider what happens when you participate in a negotiation. How do you feel about the following question (answer using either the faces or words scale)?

What's your typical motivation for entering a negotiation?

| I avoid it completely | I have no other choice | To give it a go | Because I enjoy it |

What's impacting your success in negotiations?

Think about a negotiation you have coming up. Consider what factors may hinder your success and tick them off the list below; note any extras that aren't listed.

☐ Knowing where to start   ☐ Overcome with fear

☐ I need some tactics   ☐ Feeling stressed

☐ Lacking confidence   ☐ Feeling intimidated

☐ _____   ☐ _____

You should now have more clarity on how you really feel about negotiating, and why.

By understanding your skills, capabilities and weaknesses, you will more easily shift towards being the type of negotiator you want to be, and each step you take will be the right one for you.

You may find yourself stepping out of your comfort zone at times, but it won't be uncomfortable for long. Before you know it, your confidence will be soaring as you work your way through the simple, practical activities outlined throughout this book.

But before we get started on that, let's look at some of the common reasons why so many of us don't love negotiating.

why do people hate negotiating?

Why do people hate negotiating?

Why do people hate negotiating?

It's no surprise that most of us don't like negotiating, especially considering the range of internal and external factors that influence our perception of it. In fact, a 2015 survey by Salary.com found that 87% of people surveyed are either "sometimes or always apprehensive about negotiations."

These feelings directly impact the process and the outcome of their negotiations. Not only do their negotiations end up being awkward and uncomfortable – at best – they're doomed to fail.

In a nutshell, I believe that people hate negotiating because they haven't learnt how to do it. They don't have the skills, they haven't had the practice, and they don't have anything to show for their efforts, except for perhaps a few battle scars.

As a result, people tend to avoid them altogether, or screw them up.

There are a number of factors that have influenced how we view negotiations as a society – some are from within, others are environmental. Let's look at some of these aspects in more detail.

87% of people are either sometimes or always apprehensive about negotiations.

salary.com

Internal influencing factors

Don't know where to start

We're not taught how to negotiate at school or at work, so it's not surprising that people don't know where to start. As a result, negotiations are often dreaded – and avoided. Unfortunately, if you don't know where to start, you're probably not going to start – and that's a big handbrake for successful negotiations. Throughout this book, you will learn where to start.

Overcome with fear

Fear can be paralysing in a negotiation and can stop you from even entering into the process. Most people feel nervous in a negotiation; it simply proves that the outcome of this matters to you. The reality is, you will probably always have some negotiation nerves, and that's okay.

But if your ability to think clearly and remain calm whilst negotiating something that really matters to you is hindered, you need to prepare well for that negotiation. A lack of good preparation can create a cycle of self-sabotage and confirm your pre-conceived insecurities.

For example, take asking for a pay rise during challenging economic times. Most people would baulk at the thought of asking, let alone actually approaching their boss. The fear of losing their job because of their perceived greed is overwhelming, and enough to put anyone off – if it were true. The first step is to view your salary not as a privilege, but instead as an exchange of value (of your time and effort). Next, you need to be well prepared for the conversation with your manager to ensure that you navigate the conversation with an open mindset. (Outlined later in this book.)

View your salary not as a privilege, but instead as an exchange of value

You will soon find that there really is little to fear

The more you practice negotiating, the more normal it will become, and you will soon find that there really is little to fear. Over time you will start to find that some reactions are predictable – this will eliminate the irrational fears.

Lack confidence

Without the skills and experience, it is little wonder that people site a lack of confidence as a key reason why they hate negotiating.

Cultivating the skills outlined in this book and developing negotiating as a habit will build your confidence and help you get what you want. The more you practice, the more comfortable you will feel and the more confident you will become.

Don't want to look like I need it

Pride can really get in your way when negotiating. If you are in a position where you can afford to pay full price for something, it can be uncomfortable to ask for a discount or haggle over the price for fear of looking greedy.

However, that's really not the point. Negotiating is normal and typically people don't judge you for asking the question. As long as your demeanour is positive and open, others will simply see you making a request that they may or may not be able to accommodate, simple as that.

Think it will be a fight

We often negotiate on things that matter to us – this can make the situation highly charged. However, assuming that it's going to be a fight before you even begin the discussion puts you at a significant disadvantage from the outset.

Assuming it's going to be a fight before you even begin puts you at a significant disadvantage

If you believe that a negotiation is likely to be a fight is based on your past experiences, it's likely that those experiences were actually arguments, not negotiations. Therefore, it's important to shift your mindset and be open to a discussion. You also need to recognise when others are closed to it, and consider walking away.

External influencing factors

Growing up with price tags

Most people reading this book have probably grown up in a culture where it's widely accepted that the price on the price tag is the price that you pay. There's nothing wrong with that, except at times when you're faced with a scenario where the price tag isn't fixed.

Along the way, however, price tags have become negotiable on the big ticket items – the ones that have a high degree of emotion attached to them such as buying a car or a house or negotiating a pay rise. This makes many of us feel very uncomfortable and is a significant contributor to our dislike of negotiating.

Unfortunately, it's times like these – when there is no fixed price tag – that you are at a natural disadvantage to those who have grown up in a culture where the tradition is to barter, trade or haggle over price. (More on the influence of price tags later in this chapter.)

Advertising and sales influences

We have not long emerged from years of advertising based on manipulation – telling us what we need in our lives in order to 'keep up with the Joneses'. This style of marketing was led by early advertising executives like the Don Draper types (from the TV show Mad Men) who said things like: "People want to be told what to do so badly that they'll listen to anyone."

In tandem with this type of advertising, the sales teams of old were trained in tactics that focused on creating tension and pressure to drive us to part with our money. The entire process – from planting the idea to closing the sale – was an exercise in manipulation.

It's no wonder that people find negotiating daunting and say that they hate it.

Thankfully, advertising and sales funnel processes have largely shifted. There is no longer a need to buy into a farcical dream or accept a pushy sales person in order to 'keep up with the Joneses'. We have more control and more options than ever before.

These options include the huge volume of shops we can choose to buy our items from. With the explosion of online shopping, our options are almost endless.

Time to stop being so hard on yourself

Hopefully you are beginning to understand that some of the reasons you hate negotiating have been out of your control. And that none of your personal reasons for hating it are unreasonable or irrational.

It's important to acknowledge that your thoughts, concerns and fears can be overcome with the right information and understanding.

If you want to get better at negotiating, it's time to shift your mindset by being open to a different approach. In working through this book, you will start to see a rapid change in your abilities and how you feel about negotiating.

Why do people hate negotiating?

what makes for a good negotiation?

What makes for a good negotiation?

What makes for a good negotiation?

In order to understand how to become a good negotiator, it makes sense to start by understanding the definition.

Here are a number of definitions of the word 'negotiation':

Oxford Dictionaries:

Discussion aimed at reaching an agreement.

Merriam-Webster Dictionary:

A formal discussion between people who are trying to reach an agreement.

Wikipedia:

Negotiation is a dialogue between two or more people or parties intended to reach a mutually beneficial outcome, resolve points of difference, to gain advantage for an individual or collective, or to craft outcomes to satisfy various interests.

The Law Dictionary:

The deliberation, discussion, or conference upon the terms of a proposed agreement; the act of settling or arranging the terms and conditions of a bargain, sale, or other business transaction.

So, what's the common theme?

_____

_____

HINT: It's simply about reaching an agreement, together.

Humans make negotiations messy

What the definitions fail to take into account is how the human condition affects the negotiation process. Most of us have a high degree of emotional attachment to people and objects. This attachment often gets in the way of a successful negotiation and more often than not makes negotiating messy and uncomfortable.

You probably haven't been taught how to be a good negotiator, or haven't seen best practice negotiations modelled in your family home or business, so it's natural that you may try to avoid these situations altogether.

When you're not clear on what makes for a good negotiation, you're not clear on how to get maximum value for yourself without it getting chaotic and confusing.

Perhaps you fear looking like you need a discount, or that you are 'tight'? I'm sure that's not the case. Few of us actually need a discount, but I bet you'd like one.

If you shy away from negotiating, or enter into the process ill-prepared, you are likely to walk away frustrated or disappointed by the outcome. However, if you don't negotiate at all you will almost always feel like you've been ripped off – and the little voice inside your head will wonder 'what if?'.

TICK THE BOX NEXT TO ANY OF THE SCENARIOS BELOW THAT HAVE COME UP FOR YOU IN THE PAST:

☐ When I changed jobs, I didn't push hard enough for the salary I really wanted. I feel like I got short changed.

☐ Last time I bought a car, I think I paid too much. I'm sure I got ripped off.

☐ When I tried to get additional resources for a major project at work, I was unsuccessful. I was disappointed and daunted by the project ahead.

☐ When I bought my sofa, I didn't even think about negotiating a deal. I missed an opportunity.

☐ When I purchased a computer, I did some research but ended up buying the one the salesperson recommended. I think I could have gotten a better computer or a better price.

I'm sure that one or more of these scenarios has happened to you at some point. My intention is that, after reading this book, you won't suffer that niggling feeling that you could have gotten a better deal. I don't want you to feel like you've been ripped off ever again!

Winning isn't the goal

Good negotiations are often inappropriately referred to as a win-win situation. Why is it inappropriate? Well, the sentiment is right, but the words are wrong.

On hearing words such as winning and losing, the brain switches to *fight or flight* mode where a number of reactions occur as the brain prepares to take on an opponent or to retreat – reactions that you don't want or need in the negotiation process.

When you compete to win, you have a natural need to dominate the other party. While in this state, your natural judgement system is turned down to enable the more primitive responses to take over. Your brain thinks that this is a time for action – rather than deep thought – which can lead to a negative outcome in a negotiation.

As Ricky Bobby, Will Farrell's character in the movie *Talladega Nights* summarised so well, when you are looking for a win: 'If you're not first, you're last.'

As you start negotiating more regularly you should also be mindful of the brain's addiction to being right. In a recent article, *'Your Brain is Hooked on Being Right'* by Judith E. Glaser, Chairman of The Creating WE Institute, she highlights, "When you argue and win, your brain floods with different hormones: adrenaline and dopamine, which makes you feel good, dominant, even invincible. It's a feeling any of us would want to replicate. So the next time we're in a tense situation, we fight again. We get addicted to being right."

In their book Negotiation Genius, Harvard Business School Professors Deepak Malhotra and Max H. Bazerman note that "In addition to claiming as much of the value as possible, your focus as a negotiator should also be to look at potential ways you can create value for all parties. This idea often gets lost in the pressure of trying to claim as much of the value as possible but if you can get everyone focused on finding practical ways to grow the pie [at] the same time, spectacular things can result."

A good negotiation finishes with a fair and reasonable exchange of value

I believe a good negotiation finishes with a fair and reasonable exchange of value. You may not win, you may not have had everything go your way, but you should be proud of what you've achieved and happy with what you've received, otherwise you should have walked away (more on that later).

It's not about getting what you want at all cost

In a good negotiation, you need to wake up the next day and be proud of what you've achieved. You need to feel as if you would be happy to have had your mother or your child sitting beside you as you worked towards the outcome you were looking for.

If you are desperate to win at all costs, your negotiation is bound to go sideways and it is unlikely that the other party will ever want to deal with you again. Also, you are unlikely to be proud of yourself.

It's not about screwing the other guy on price. If you end up pushing so hard that the other person feels like they've been robbed, that's not fair or reasonable.

Be considerate, fair and respectful

Buying something at a rock-bottom price is fine if you are an average negotiator, but to be a good negotiator, you need to consider the other party's needs and values.

This is especially important when you're dealing with other cultures; for example, in Thailand, a great way to get an awesome deal is to get to the markets early – aim to be their first sale of the day.

Why? In Thai culture, if they close the first sale of the day, it is considered good luck for the rest of their sales day. The salesperson will be desperate for you not to walk away without a purchase. In this situation you face a moral dilemma: do you screw them on price because you can or do you give them fair and reasonable value?

You're not buying from a big company with big margins, your money is going into that family's pocket; but, still you have two options:

1. You could go for it, and get a killer deal. They may have good luck for the rest of the day, but that first sale has hurt them financially. Making their starting point at 'break even' or worse they may have lost money on the first sale of the day. That's not fair or reasonable.

2. The alternate option is to haggle with them as much as you can, but stay alert. You will notice when their face changes, when the laughter stops. That's a tell-tale sign that they aren't going to make any money. If this happens, take a step backward, offer them the last price you suggested before the smiles stopped and close the deal. To me, that's fair and reasonable – and fun!

What makes for a good negotiation?

What makes for a good negotiation?

why improve your skills now?

Why improve your skills now?

Why do you need to get good at negotiating now? You've always managed to fumble your way through negotiations to date, so why change now?

- The way deals are being done is changing.
- The world of business – from the smallest one-man operation to the biggest corporation – is shifting.

As a result, now more than ever, you need to develop your negotiating skills.

Shifting behaviours — value exchange

Before price tags were invented (about 150 years ago), everyone bartered or traded and both parties would eventually agree upon what something was worth. That is, an item or service would only be worth what someone was prepared to 'pay' for it.

In recent years, price tags have ruled and I would argue that we have become a little too reliant on them. This has led to us losing our negotiation skills along the way.

But the rise and rise of auction sites such as eBay and GraysOnline (and many others like them) have rekindled the relationship between what we think something is worth, and what someone in the market is prepared to pay for it.

To be clear, auctions are not negotiations, but the proliferation of this new retail model has driven a collective mindset shift in relation to how we purchase things, and how we value our money.

Rise of the service economy

For the first time since before the industrial revolution, serviced-based organisations are outperforming product-based companies on the stock market worldwide. Now, more than ever, it is imperative that businesses view customers as being at the heart of everything they do.

The golden age of pushy advertising and sales tactics that told us what we needed is over. Smart companies are now training their salespeople differently and are having conversations about the customer experience and how they can improve it. They want us to leave their stores or their website having had a positive experience. They want us to feel that we have been part of a genuine exchange for fair and reasonable value. These are the companies that we enjoy dealing with and these are the companies that will flourish into the future.

This shift gives buyers more opportunities to negotiate a better deal with ease as sellers are more open.

Generational shifts

Parallel to these shifts, the next generation of leaders view their personal value very differently to the generations before them. This in turn impacts the way they think about money.

When I was younger, I heard a Gen Y colleague tell our manager that she had "reached capacity" in response to him asking her to do something extra for him. At the time I was shocked and I thought she was being lazy. Hell, all of us have reached capacity, just suck it up!

But I soon realised she was 100 per cent right: in order to deliver effectively on his expectations, she would have to drop something, and he needed to know that. We had all reached capacity some time ago; I just didn't know how to articulate it, while she did.

Needless to say, she taught me a lot, including a healthy respect for how Gen Y workers view their value.

Where once an employee would simply work harder and longer to deliver outcomes, the next generations are saying that we must work smarter and respect the investment of our time in exchange for a reasonable day's pay.

The revolution is upon us

Price tags may never become obsolete in our society, but they are becoming more and more targeted to commoditised items only. So, it's time for a negotiation revolution.

We must all learn this skill. I truly hope that the education disruption that is underway worldwide will include this life skill in the new raft

> It's time for a negotiation revolution

of essentials we must teach our children. Meanwhile, for those who don't want to be left behind, this book is for you.

It's time for all of us to get comfortable with negotiating. It's a bit like computers: if you grew up in the pre-computer era you might have understandably been hesitant to embrace them. But the sooner you did, the sooner they became part of your life. And the sooner you reaped the benefits.

how to shift your mindset

How to shift your mindset

Your mindset is a huge influence on how you negotiate. It's been shaped by your experiences and it influences your confidence. But it's not set in stone, and it isn't too late to change it.

In Dr Carol Dweck's book *Mindset: The New Psychology of Success* she explains how influential our mindsets are on what we want and how we will get it. In her years of research on the subject, Dr Dweck observed the existence of two types of minds – growth and fixed. She talks about how some of us get stuck in a fixed mindset unwilling to change and some of us have a growth mindset continuously learning, growing and changing.

With regard to negotiating, she asks the question, "Are good negotiators born or made?" In response, she references other research in this area: "… researchers Laura Kray and Michael Haselhuhn have shown that people in a growth mindset make better negotiators. They also found that when business school students were taught a growth mindset they learned more skills and got better grades in their negotiation course. Negotiators with a growth mindset were much more able to push past obstacles and reach an agreement that benefited both sides."

You may have an open mindset to many things in life, yet you can still be closed to others (such as negotiating). Essentially, it's your choice.

In order to shift to a growth mindset on this subject, you should also consider the 'baggage' you carry around with you: your association with money, and how confident you are with it.

In Susan Wahhab's book *Money Intelligence* she notes that "We learn Money Intelligence at home. These are the money values our parents teach us, or model to us, that get imprinted in our minds. Those values influence our acquired and learnt mindset that end up shaping our destiny."

If the way we think about money has been shaped for years and years, it stands to reason that how we think about negotiating has been developing over this period as well.

But, like anything, with the desire, and with practice, you can embrace a theory and develop it into a habit that works for you.

Negotiation is a learned skill, even if it's one we didn't learn at home or at school. And, as with all good learning, it's important to put concepts into practice. Once you are taught how, the more you practice and the more you view negotiations with a growth mindset, the more your confidence will build. You will become more self-assured and more comfortable talking about money and asking for what you want.

There is a lot going on in your brain that impacts your mindset towards negotiations. By deconstructing this myriad of influences, and then building a growth mindset towards negotiation, you will find that you will be able to approach and manage negotiations with more confidence and ease. The activities in this book will help you make the mindset shift you need.

The melting pot of things contributing to your negotiation growth mindset

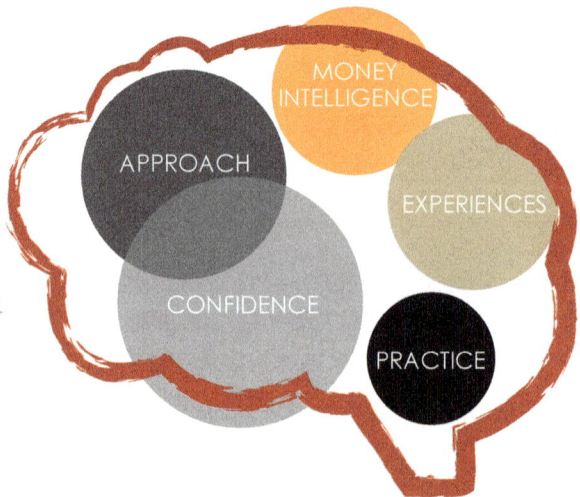

MONEY INTELLIGENCE

APPROACH

EXPERIENCES

CONFIDENCE

PRACTICE

what type of negotiator are you?

What type of negotiator are you?

In order to understand how best to develop your specific set of negotiation skills, we first need to establish what type of negotiator you are.

Questions to understand what type of negotiator you are

The following questionnaire is designed to assess where you are on the scale of negotiation mastery, with a view to understanding what skills you are already comfortable with and where there is room for growth.

Simply read through each statement and note down how aligned you feel you are with each message.

Answer the questions as the negotiator you are today, not the one you want to be.

My intention is that, by the time you finish working through this book, you will have evolved into a more confident and capable negotiator and will have moved up the scale.

Read through each of these questions, consider them and rate how you feel about them. Make sure you give each statement some thought, paying attention to how you react when you read it.

USE THIS SCALE TO CONFIRM YOUR POSITION:

1	2	3	4
Completely disagree	Disagree	Agree	Strongly agree

STATEMENT	SCORE 1 – 4
I get excited by the thought of negotiating.	
When there is an opportunity to negotiate I happily take on the challenge.	
I am comfortable talking about money in any situation.	
I do a lot of research before making any significant purchase.	
I negotiated my last pay rise and was very happy with the outcome.	
I happily call in favours from others if I think they can help me in a negotiation.	
I am generally successful when I negotiate.	
I typically feel in control during a negotiation.	
I have a game plan for each negotiation I enter.	
When given an unrealistic deadline from my manager I'm happy to negotiate a better one.	

STATEMENT	SCORE 1 - 4
When I renewed the contract for my last electricity bill I played one supplier off another to get a good deal.	
I think through conversations or scenarios that may come up during a negotiation to increase my chances of success.	
I made a counter-offer when I was told the price of the last car I bought.	
I never pay the price on the price tag.	
I never hesitate to ask for a little more of anything.	

ADD UP YOUR TOTAL

Now it's time to total your score and move to the next section of the book to understand what type of negotiator you are.

negotiator profiles

Negotiator profiles

Your negotiator profile

Over many years working on deals at all levels of investment, both financial and personal, I have observed that there are four typical negotiator profiles.

My 'scale of negotiation mastery' shows how people's level of mastery is influenced by two key factors: your DESIRE to participate in a negotiation (voluntarily) and your INTEREST in the outcome (what might be).

As your mindset and skill levels shift, your confidence will grow, and your DESIRE to participate in negotiations will increase. Concurrently, as you see more positive results, your INTEREST in the outcome will naturally heighten.

Understanding your profile will help you focus your efforts on the skills you may not yet be confident with and on the tactics you may not even know exist – this should help you move through the tiers of mastery.

So, where do you sit on the scale of negotiation mastery? Your profile's typical mindset is revealed below. A full description of each profile is in the pages that follow.

YOUR SCORE	YOUR PROFILE	GO TO PAGE
15-25	AVOIDER	page 54
25-40	DABBLER	page 56
40-50	ADVENTURER	page 58
50-60	MASTERY	page 60

Profile 1

THE AVOIDER

If you are simply too scared to even try your hand at negotiating, you are an Avoider. In my world, this is my mum. I love her to bits but, bless her, she's so nice she doesn't want to upset anyone.

She is not comfortable, confident or interested in negotiating, so she actively does not engage in any negotiation situation.

Like all good Avoiders, she'd prefer it if everything she wanted to buy had a price tag. Even if that means she's paying too much.

Avoiders need a mindset makeover. Negotiating isn't about being mean or being nice – it's a business transaction, a value exchange. It's about getting a good deal for you, and not getting ripped off.

PROFILE	AVOIDER
CONFIDENCE	Agonised
MINDSET	Make it stop!
RESULTS	Risk being ripped off

Things you will be negotiating confidently at the end of this book

We just want to get you started, so you will be negotiating smaller items such as whitegoods. These are basic items you can easily Google the best price for, then visit a shop that is open to negotiation and give it a go. Simple, simple, simple.

You are currently a salesman's dream... time for a change

Objectives from this book

Perhaps you will never love negotiating, but this book should build your confidence, reduce the stress associated with it and shift you to a mindset where you at least want to dabble a little more regularly. As a result, you will progress to become a Dabbler.

Avoider, we need to get you in the game, so try negotiating for things like fruit and vegies or small appliances.

Where to from here

In the next section of this book, you will walk through the four stages of a negotiation (more about these shortly). As you go through the stages, I have created a series of activities specifically aimed at your current negotiation skill level.

ALL AVOIDER ACTIVITIES IN THIS BOOK ARE COLOURED GREY.

Profile 2

THE DABBLER

If you find yourself wanting to enter into the negotiation process, but you're a little scared and unsure, then you are a Dabbler.

It is likely that you are confident in your day job, but lack confidence in negotiation situations. You probably just don't really know how to go about the process. You don't want to make an offer that is perceived as being rude or offensive. Or perhaps you don't want to look tight or like you need a discount.

You will occasionally give it a shot, asking for a discount and receive a few dollars off here and there. But even in the process of asking for this discount, you might try and talk the salesperson out of it, embarrassed that you asked (ever uttered the words 'Oh, it's OK, don't worry about it'?).

You will engage in negotiations when you need to, but you find the whole thing very stressful. HOWEVER, you are keen to become a better negotiator, so you have a great deal of growth ahead.

For you, it's time to build on your positive experiences and create an approach that works for you every time.

PROFILE	DABBLER
CONFIDENCE	Awkward
MINDSET	Please sir, can I have some more?
RESULTS	Hit and miss

Time to put both feet in the water, with confidence

Things you will be negotiating confidently at the end of this book

It's time to get involved in negotiations that really matter, such as purchasing a car, obtaining a pay rise or entering into similarly stressful or important negotiations.

Objectives from this book

The information you're about to receive will boost your confidence and arm you with tactics you can implement daily. You will continue to feel more comfortable with negotiating, achieve some great outcomes along the way and progress to become an Adventurer.

Dabbler, you need to understand a little more about your emotional reactions. I want to help you manage your emotions, read the play and trust your gut. Think big, be brave.

Where to from here

In the next section of this book, you will walk through the four stages of a negotiation (more about these shortly). As you go through the stages, I have created a series of activities specifically aimed at your current negotiation skill level.

ALL DABBLER ACTIVITIES IN THIS BOOK ARE COLOURED ORANGE.

Profile 3

THE ADVENTURER

You are starting to make negotiating part of your world every day. Perhaps it's a skill you need for your job? You get involved regularly, but there's still room for you to grow. You are an Adventurer.

It is likely that you are heavily focused on getting the best price when you're at the negotiating table. However, you may be leaving some things on the table. Sometimes you have a niggling feeling that you ought to have been able to get a better deal, a feeling that you could have gotten more.

You may also occasionally feel you pushed a little too hard. You might wake up feeling bad that the other party wasn't happy at the end of the process. They weren't smiling when you walked away. You got a great price, but it may have been at the expense of the other guy instead of reaching the best deal for everyone.

It's time to work on your approach strategies which will see you jump the final hurdle into negotiation mastery. It's about learning to play the game a little differently.

PROFILE	ADVENTURER
CONFIDENCE	Comfortable
MINDSET	I deserve what I get
RESULTS	Mostly positive

Ensure you see the signs, so you don't miss any opportunities

Things you will be negotiating confidently at the end of this book

You will be confident enough to negotiate complex purchases, such as a new house build and commercial deals that are bound up in lots of intricacies.

Objectives from this book

You're probably starting to love negotiating, but can have mixed results. As a consequence, sometimes you love it but sometimes you smart from the experience. This book will help you to consistently enjoy the process and get the most out of any opportunities, while building your reputation as a serious player in the negotiation landscape.

Where to from here

In the next section of this book, you will walk through the four stages of a negotiation (more about these shortly). As you go through the stages, I have created a series of activities specifically aimed at your current negotiation skill level.

ALL ADVENTURER ACTIVITIES IN THIS BOOK ARE COLOURED BLUE.

Profile 4
THE MASTER

Congratulations! If you are a negotiation Master it is likely that you regularly need this skill in your job. You, like me, should love negotiating (if not, perhaps it's time for a new job).

I think it would be a little inappropriate for me to school you in a skill you are already proficient at, so I have omitted building a series of activities for the Masters.

However, as with any pursuit, once you have reached mastery it is your obligation to share your knowledge. You will be looking for opportunities to grow, and the best way to do this is to teach others.

Imparting your knowledge will remind you of what you're good at, and give you a chance to learn a few new tricks from those you teach.

PROFILE	MASTER
CONFIDENCE	Fearless
MINDSET	What's the best strategy?
RESULTS	Good deal for all

"If you're lucky enough
to do well, it's your
responsibility to send the
elevator back down."

Kevin Spacey

Things you will be negotiating confidently at the end of this book

Anything at all, it's likely that this is your job or a regular part of it. I look forward to working with you some time.

Objectives from this book

I'd like to invite you to expand the negotiation revolution by helping others move through the tiers of confidence. As in these delightful words of Kevin Spacey:

four stages for a good negotiation

Four stages for a good negotiation

These are the four stages that make up every good negotiation:

Your first choice is to **ACCEPT** that this is happening. You are going to actively become involved in (more) negotiations. This is solely your choice.

ACCEPT

To make the negotiation process as effortless as possible it's important that you **PREPARE**. You are probably doing some of this already, as it starts with your online research, but there is a lot more you can do.

PREPARE

It's time to get involved, time to **ENGAGE** in a negotiation – this is where the fun starts. By now you have everything you need, so it's time to get involved – go for it!

ENGAGE

Now that you are in the negotiation, it's time to **CLOSE**. In straightforward deals, this is a natural part of the process – typically when you hand over the cash, but there are a few tricks of the trade you can learn here to get the best deal during the final stages of the negotiation.

CLOSE

Tailored activities so you learn to love it!

This section of the book is your adventure. You choose which exercises you take for a spin. I recommend you kick off at the point aligned with your negotiation profile, but feel free to jump to others if they suit a situation or negotiation you are currently preparing for or experiencing.

The key thing is to have fun with it. This is your workbook, so make it work for you. Write in it and on it. Note down in the space provided what didn't work, what you enjoyed, what made you feel icky, and what worked!

Please don't give up. If you are an Avoider, a lot of this is foreign territory so why not work on your negotiations with a buddy? Shop with someone else for a little bit of moral support. If they are an Avoider too, perhaps you could encourage one another. If it isn't working, try buddying up with a Dabbler, and so on.

Working through each of the stages and activities

Each section begins with an overview of the theory of that stage of the negotiation. After that, there are specific activities for each negotiation profile. To make it easy to navigate, at the top of each activity it notes which profile should start with that particular activity. It's totally your choice to work through all of the activities, or simply focus on the ones aligned to your profile.

At the bottom of each activity there are a couple of things for you to note down to help you become more proficient at each skill:

☐ **GAVE IT A GO**

Tick the box once you 'Gave it a go'. Then make notes on what worked, what didn't and what you can try next time.

☐ **GOT IT**

Continue working on the activity, building off what you learn along the way until you feel confident enough to tick the box that you've 'Got it!'

Once you've got it, it's time to move to the next activity. This is your adventure, so feel free to traverse back and forward through the activities, until you are comfortable. I highly recommend you make notes as you work through it, that way when you come back to an activity you will remember where you left off.

As you work through these activities you are likely to be feeling uncomfortable from time to time, and you may experience a few emotions you weren't expecting. Rest assured, these feelings will pass.

In Jenny Brockis' book *Future Brain* she explains how "Emotion is crucial to learning: We make around 30,000 decisions every day, many of which are subconscious and all of which incorporate our emotions... Our emotions play an important role in all our thoughts and actions. We are moved mainly by emotion, not logic."

She goes on to talk about how "Emotion and memory are very strongly intertwined. That's because in a heightened level of stress our amygdala [part of the brain responsible for emotions, survival instincts and memory] becomes hyperactive and enhances those memories with a strong emotional component, while activity in the hippocampus, the area of the brain associated with learning and memory, decreases."

SUMMARY OF ALL ACTIVITIES

Here is a summary of all the activities for all the profiles. While it is advised that you work through the activities for your profile type in the order outlined below, there will be times that you may need help in a specific situation. In that case, use this table as a reference to jump back and forth throughout the book.

SECTION	ACTIVITY	PROFILE
ACCEPT		
Time to accept	Awakening	AVOIDER
	Become more aware	DABBLER
PREPARE		
Research pays off	The basics	AVOIDER
	Background check	DABBLER
	Use your network	ADVENTURER
How much to pay	Align your head & heart	AVOIDER
	A matter of priorities	DABBLER
What's your game plan	Visualise it	AVOIDER
	Talk it through	DABBLER
	Write a plan (to get a pay rise)	ADVENTURER
ENGAGE		
Play the game	Don't ask, Don't get	AVOIDER
	Fake it, 'til you make it	DABBLER
	Price beat not price match please	DABBLER
	Push it	ADVENTURER
Nerves mean it matters	Managing your nerves	AVOIDER
	Break it down	DABBLER
	Slow down, no rush	ADVENTURER

SECTION	ACTIVITY	PROFILE
Read the play	Trust your gut	AVOIDER
	Body language	DABBLER
	The wry smile	ADVENTURER
Manage your emotions	Face your fears	AVOIDER
	FOMO Tactics	DABBLER
	Stop the backflips	DABBLER
	Don't lose your head	ADVENTURER
Managing challenges	Take the heat out	DABBLER
	It's not personal!	DABBLER
	Call it	ADVENTURER
	Wear a different hat	ADVENTURER
	Give them an out	ADVENTURER
	A neutral advisor	ADVENTURER

CLOSE

SECTION	ACTIVITY	PROFILE
Time is your friend	Time's best friend	AVOIDER
	Types of time-out	DABBLER
	Time of year, month, day	ADVENTURER
Show me the money	Rip the Band-Aid	AVOIDER
	Don't negotiate with yourself	DABBLER
	Don't go too far	ADVENTURER
Know when to fold 'em	Just say 'no thanks'	AVOIDER
	Not good enough	DABBLER
	Value misalignment	ADVENTURER
The last word	The last word	ALL

Stage 1

IT'S HAPPENING –
TIME TO ACCEPT

ACCEPT

Time to accept

The first stage is to ACCEPT that this is happening – you are going to enter into a negotiation. You will actively participate in a negotiation, until which time you choose not to. It's as simple as that.

In the process of acceptance, however, I suggest changing the way you look at your upcoming negotiation, to help ensure that it is as stress-free as possible.

Negotiating is simply a series of choices. Think of it as being like a bus ride: it's best to know where you want to go before you hail the bus. And if it doesn't feel like it's going in the right direction, you can choose to stop and get off any time you like. But, before you can go anywhere, you need to make the decision to hail the bus.

As you embark on this series of choices, you may also want to accept that it might be a little awkward from time to time, but it will definitely be worth it once you come out the other side with a positive result.

So, let's hail that bus...

AWAKENING

STRATEGY   TIME TO ACCEPT

PROFILE   AVOIDER

ACCEPT

OVERVIEW

- As an Avoider, your first step is to make a conscious choice to participate in a negotiation.
- The thought of negotiating probably fills you with dread, but if you do it and get a positive result, you will be so proud of yourself (and you'll have something good to show for it).
- I'm sure you negotiate all the time without any major issues, but it happens without you even noticing you are doing it.
- This activity is passive and one you can do relatively quietly and discreetly.

ACTION PART 1 RAISE YOUR AWARENESS

It's time to become more aware.

Over the next week, tick off what you do from this list:

- [ ] Debated what to have for dinner with your partner
- [ ] Agreed which movie to see with a friend
- [ ] Selected a venue for an event you are attending on the weekend
- [ ] At work, fixed a time for a meeting in a very busy diary
- [ ] Pushed back on a deadline or request
- [ ] Considered having dessert, but talked yourself out of it

All these activities involve an element of negotiating and you are probably better at it than you give yourself credit for.

Continued over the page ☞

AWAKENING (CONTINUED)

As you are developing this skill, it's important for you to spend time taking notice of how you feel and how you react during these interactions. Note these down below.

Be aware and note how you react when things get tough. Also, it might be enlightening to note when you find some activities easy.

My feelings:

_____

_____

_____

_____

My reactions:

_____

_____

_____

_____

Activities I found pretty easy:

_____

_____

_____

The more conscious you are that you can negotiate, and the more you become aware of what emotions, feelings and thoughts come up for you during negotiations, the more comfortable you will become with them over time.

ACTION PART 2 A NEW APPROACH

Once you have identified the activities that you find easiest, it's time to try being a bit more forward, or approach conversations in a more forthright manner. Perhaps say to the other person that it's important to you to get what you want. **Simply ask for a little more or a little less and see what happens**.

You could tell your partner or best friend that you are keen to improve you negotiation skills, so they can help you practice, give you feedback and play the game with you.

Each interaction will help make you a better, more confident negotiator. Keep working through your list until you are feeling confident with the majority of them.

☐ GAVE IT A GO

Actions for next time

_____

_____

_____

_____

Notes

_____

_____

_____

_____

_____

☐ GOT IT

BECOME MORE AWARE

STRATEGY   TIME TO ACCEPT

PROFILE   DABBLER

OVERVIEW

There are opportunities to negotiate every day, and your task at this stage is to notice them and action them.

ACTION

As you wander through your day, start actively looking for more opportunities to negotiate. Think about all the shops you enter and what's possible. Consider the meetings or situations you are in every day and where there may be opportunities for you to actively participate in negotiations as they come up.

Perhaps ask for an extra resource for a project, or an extra doughnut when you order 10 (ask for a bulk-buy discount!). **Ask to pay a little less here, or to get a little more there**.

The point is that you are accepting that there are more opportunities than you may have previously noticed. It's not about the outcome - it really doesn't matter if you end up with nothing. Just say thank you and move on.

The point is that you are starting to ask for a little more. The more accepting you are, the more confident you will be, which will help you when a negotiation really matters to you.

☐ GAVE IT A GO

Actions for next time

ACCEPT

Notes

☐ GOT IT

Stage 2:
DON'T GO IN BLIND – LET'S PREPARE

PREPARE

If you want a positive outcome, you need to PREPARE for every negotiation. The more complex and important the subject of your negotiation becomes, the more thorough and essential your preparation needs to be.

It doesn't have to be an overly complicated process but, if you go in blind, you might baulk at the first hurdle along the way, and that hurts your confidence and leads to disappointment.

To keep it simple, if you run through the following sequence every time you head towards a negotiation, you will feel more in control and ultimately more confident.

Preparation Strategies

1. **Research pays off**
2. **How much to pay**
3. **What's your game plan**

Strategy: Research pays off

For straightforward purchases, online research is the first place to look for direct comparisons on price. You can do all the legwork before you even leave the house.

The effort you expend on this desk research will contribute to building your confidence for any negotiation, as you will start out in an educated and strong position.

PREPARE

You should also consider who you know and how your relationships can help you get a better deal. Maybe someone mentioned they got a good deal on something you are looking to buy. Why not give that contact a call? Referrals are a great start to consider who you might like to give your money to.

Attempt something new every week, just small things, and don't think too much about it. Try to detach your feelings from the outcome.

Try to detach your feelings from the outcome

ACTIVITIES: RESEARCH PAYS OFF

The Basics	page 80
Background check	page 82
Use your network	page 84

PREPARE

Strategy: How much to pay

This is the question we all want to know, right? Well, the answer to that question depends on you.

There are many ways to reveal this answer. But the reality is, it's about how much you value something. There's truth in the old adage that the price is only what someone is willing to pay. If something is highly valued by you, then it stands to reason that you will be happy to pay more.

So, it's important to spend time during your preparation to determine how much this particular item or outcome means to you.

The price is only what someone is willing to pay

ACTIVITIES: HOW MUCH TO PAY

Align your head and heart	page 86
A matter of priorities	page 88

PREPARE

Strategy: What's your game plan

There is just one more step to PREPARE you for your negotiation: get a game plan.

Every situation is different, and you can't pre-empt everything, but it's always preferable to have a game plan. It will help you enjoy the process because you will have taken the time to think through how the negotiation might go. You'll feel much better prepared, and much less stressed.

ACTIVITIES: WHAT'S YOUR GAME PLAN

Visualise it	page 90
Talk it through	page 92
Write a plan (to get a pay rise)	page 94

THE BASICS

STRATEGY	RESEARCH PAYS OFF
PROFILE	AVOIDER

OVERVIEW

Simply 'Google it' up in readiness for heading out to a store.

ACTION

Decide on something you want to purchase over the next month.

Do as much online research as possible.

Learn about the different models and options available.

If you are so inclined, start a spreadsheet to **note down aspects that are important**, such as:

- the listed price
- specifications that matter to you
- which stores have which price
- additional value-adds (e.g. longer warranty, extra parts).

This will help keep you mind clear of the details, so you keep a track on what you are comparing and can refer back to it as you do more investigating, otherwise, you might find yourself a little overwhelmed.

Next, find out which of these companies have physical stores. Their website should say if they are open to negotiating on price. If this isn't clear, give them a call and just ask. It will only take you a minute to find out if their prices are negotiable. Their answer will simply be yes or no, then you hang up – easy!

They might say they are happy to offer discounts for cash. Note – 'cash' simply means you're not paying with credit, you don't have to carry a wedge of folded money with you.

All this research will help you identify from the get-go if the first sales person you speak to is genuine or trying to take the mickey out of you.

Be aware

When items are highly competitive the retailers
are likely to make it difficult for you to do a direct
comparison.

For example, I recently bought a new laptop (to write
this book) and when I was conducting my research
phase I nearly sent myself crazy trying to find a direct comparison
from each of the retailers in order to pit them against each other
to get the best price. Alas, it was just not possible. Why? I started
to notice that the configurations for each of the HP computers, for
example, were different. One store had 4GB with a touchscreen and
128SSD when another store had 4GB with no touchscreen and a
128SSD – it was so frustrating until I worked out that they are making it
impossible so there will be no such thing as a price match. They have
(cleverly) negotiated their own deals with the manufacturer, so each
is the only company with that particular configuration. It's genius
really! But annoying for anyone trying to carry out a comparison.

So, how do you deal with it? Well, I simply went about it with a white-
label approach. What would I need if I could build the laptop I
really wanted? I developed a list of must-haves and then found the
appropriate solution to fit my 'problem'.

☐ *GAVE IT A GO*

Actions for next time

_____

_____

_____

Notes

_____

_____

_____

☐ *GOT IT*

BACKGROUND CHECK

STRATEGY	RESEARCH PAYS OFF
PROFILE	DABBLER

OVERVIEW

Naturally, the more complicated the deal, the more complex your research becomes, so it's time to think about your options.

ACTION

It's time for a little investigative research. Consider a negotiation you have coming up. Run a bit of a 'background check' on those you are going to engage with. OK, not like a police check, but a check using all your available data nonetheless. Here are a few options:

- Look at online reviews and forums. What are other people saying?
- Do you know someone who has purchased the item you are about to? Ask them for a referral and information about the deal they struck.
- Conduct a LinkedIn search to understand the other party's level of experience.
- LinkedIn can also indicate any connections you have in common. Reach out to your mutual contact and learn about them, their style and any other details you can find out that might influence your chances of success prior to engaging with the other party.

☐ GAVE IT A GO

Actions for next time

_____

_____

_____

_____

_____

_____

PREPARE

Notes

_____

_____

_____

_____

_____

_____

_____

_____

_____

_____

_____

_____

_____

_____

_____

☐ GOT IT

USE YOUR NETWORK

STRATEGY	RESEARCH PAYS OFF
PROFILE	ADVENTURER

OVERVIEW

Over time you build up a pretty big network of contacts, and every now and then it's important to lean on those who you have a few favours banked with.

ACTION

While you prepare for your next big negotiation, take some time to consider who you know that works for the company or team you are about to negotiate with. Note down anything you would like their help with, or questions they may be able to answer for you, that will help build your confidence or put you in a stronger position.

Depending on your negotiation, these thought-starters might help:

- Would it help to know what the person/company likes/dislikes (similar to information you might need for an interview)?
- Can your contact give you an introduction to a key decision-maker or someone who is in a position to give you a good deal?
- Can your contact put in a good word for you?

If you have a number of people who can help out, make sure you are asking each of them different things, and that you are asking them about the most relevant thing or aspect of the business that they can help you with.

Be mindful of balance. Don't always go to the same people for help, and don't only go to these people when you need help. And finally, pay it forward. When you are thanking them for their help, open the door for them to call in the favour when they need it in future.

☐ GAVE IT A GO

Actions for next time

_____

_____

_____

_____

_____

_____

Notes

_____

_____

_____

_____

_____

_____

_____

_____

_____

_____

_____

_____

_____

_____

☐ GOT IT

ALIGN YOUR HEAD AND HEART

STRATEGY	HOW MUCH TO PAY
PROFILE	AVOIDER

OVERVIEW

It's time to take both the head and the heart's point of view into consideration and determine which one has a stronger case.

ACTION

Note down:

What's your budget?

- Is it fixed or do you have a 'budget' and a 'real budget'? Write down both.
- Why do you want this?
- What will you do with it?
- What will change if you have it?

_____

_____

_____

How much does it mean to you to have it?

- On a scale of 1 to 10, how much do you want this item or outcome?

_____

_____

_____

If you don't get it, is there an alternative you'll be happy with?

- If not, will you be terribly disappointed and potentially regret not acquiring it now?
- What does success look like?

PREPARE

_____

_____

_____

Being clear about the above will help you know how much you truly value something, so you can make a more 'planned' decision before you enter into the negotiation.

☐ GAVE IT A GO

Actions for next time

_____

_____

_____

Notes

_____

_____

_____

_____

_____

☐ GOT IT

A MATTER OF PRIORITIES

STRATEGY	HOW MUCH TO PAY
PROFILE	DABBLER

OVERVIEW

The more complex the deal, the more you need to prioritise. What do you WANT versus what do you NEED in the deal?

ACTION

Think about an upcoming negotiation that has multiple options, perhaps buying a car or house.

Make a list of everything you want in your ideal home/car/other. You may want to work on this with your partner and anyone else who this purchase will affect. **Write a big list**. Don't limit your thinking, this is ideal-scenario thinking, where money is no object.

My Priorities:

_____

_____

_____

_____

Once you have a comprehensive understanding of what you want in an ideal world, it's time to identify where you have flexibility – what you want versus what you need.

WARNING: you may say everything is a MUST HAVE; however, if you ever watched the TV show Location, Location, Location you will know that those who have spent years looking for property without buying anything are the ones with no points of compromise. If everything is a 'must have' you can potentially waste a whole lot of time and energy. Unless money really is no object, it's time to begin prioritising your list.

To do this, take your list and mark-up which items are:

- Non-negotiables – the things you cannot live without, the things you really need to satisfy the basic need you are trying to meet
- High priority – what you need that will make you happy
- Low priority – what you can live without but you want.

Be ruthless. Try to have less than three non-negotiables as these are the things that would lead you to walk away from the negotiation if the other party couldn't satisfy them.

It's also a time to be a little creative. Consider what could be added later or purchased separately to meet your requirements.

Once you have your prioritised list, you should revisit your budget and decide if it's realistic. You may find yourself reviewing your list many times as you go through the planning process, adjusting as required, but having it as a starting point should ensure that you get what you need, and hopefully more than a little of what you want.

☐ *GAVE IT A GO*

Actions for next time

_____

_____

_____

Notes

_____

_____

_____

_____

☐ *GOT IT*

VISUALISE IT

STRATEGY	WHAT'S YOUR GAME PLAN
PROFILE	AVOIDER

PREPARE

OVERVIEW

It's time to think about how it might all go down.

ACTION

Set aside some time to think through how the interaction will play out. Depending on your level of comfort, you may want to visit the store before you even have the conversation, so you can get a feel for it.

Then, talk through your approach with a friend. Between you, banter a little bit about how the conversation might go. Role-play the conversation. How will you start the conversation? What might they say and what will you say next?

☐ GAVE IT A GO

Actions for next time

_____

_____

_____

_____

_____

_____

Notes

_____

_____

_____

_____

_____

_____

_____

_____

_____

_____

_____

_____

_____

☐ *GOT IT*

TALK IT THROUGH

STRATEGY	WHAT'S YOUR GAME PLAN
PROFILE	DABBLER

PREPARE

OVERVIEW

Let's say you are about to enter into a negotiation with your manager or another department at work, where the outcome is fundamental to you meeting your KPIs or targets for the year. It's important, so you need to be ready for what might come up during the discussion.

ACTION

Be really clear about what you want from the outcome of the discussion. Write this down. Keep it single-minded.

_____

_____

_____

_____

_____

_____

Now, talk to three people about it:

- Your partner or someone who will be totally honest with you.
- One of your parents, whoever is the most objective.
- Your mentor or someone in a similar role to the person you're about to negotiate with.

In each conversation, break down your case, talk about it from all angles. Consider it from the other person's perspective. **Exhaust the conversation so it doesn't have much emotion left in it**.

After the conversations, write an action plan and commit to a timeframe to get things done. Then go do it! Make sure you go back to those who helped you and tell them about your progress. They will help bolster your confidence if things take longer than you want.

☐ **GAVE IT A GO**

Actions for next time

_____

_____

_____

_____

Notes

_____

_____

_____

_____

_____

_____

_____

_____

_____

☐ **GOT IT**

WRITE A PLAN (TO GET A PAY RISE)

STRATEGY WHAT'S YOUR GAME PLAN

PROFILE ADVENTURER

OVERVIEW

If you are about to negotiate something that is highly important to you, and you have an emotional attachment to it, it's crucial to have a written plan.

ACTION

According to a 2015 survey by salary.com, **59% of people dread salary negotiations** because it causes feelings of nervousness and apprehension. So, if you are headed into a salary negotiation for a new job, or your current job, it's important to have a written plan. This can be simple and it's not something you need to give to the other party. It could be as basic as having a script to use if you're nervous. Your plan will help keep you focused and on topic, particularly when times get tough in the conversation.

Here are six things to consider in your plan:

1. Prepare the scene. Ensure there are no surprises by creating the best opportunity for this conversation to succeed.

- Make sure your manager knows the purpose of the meeting in advance. Instead of asking for a meeting about a pay rise, **change the conversation from the get-go: ask for a meeting to discuss your value in the company.** This will help them understand that you are talking 'big picture'.

- Pick a time/day that they are typically quiet; if something major comes up, move your meeting.

- Consider what they might say or how they may react. Remember, managers are rarely trained in how to handle situations like this, so they get nervous too. Brainstorm this with people managers you know, your mentor and someone who knows your manager. Have notes ready to help guide your response to these potential reactions.

2. Know your end goal.

- What's your compromise position, ideal state and perfect world?

- What will you do if you don't get what you want? Really consider this as it will help to clarify your boundaries.

PREPARE

---

3. Be clear on why you're entitled to this.

- Managers can't give you an increase because you've been there for a long time, because they like you, or because of your lifestyle choices. Something has to have changed: more responsibility, more staff, covering a bigger geographic area, for example.

- Create a comparison of your current job description and what you actually do.

- Get a copy of your company's policy for pay increases and be clear on the rules and timing for increases.

- Change the conversation. When you are talking about a pay rise, introduce language about your value and what you are worth in the business. This will change it from simply talking about money – it's about what's fair and reasonable.

Continued over the page ☞

WRITE A PLAN (TO GET A PAY RISE)

PREPARE

4. Think for the person you are negotiating with.

• Are they the decision maker? If not, consider how you can help them sell your case up the chain.

• What alternatives to cash are available? Could they give you additional leave, an increased bonus, shorter working hours, a car space, fewer staff or additional training?

_____

_____

_____

_____

_____

5. Keep calm and be patient.

• The process is likely to take weeks (12 weeks on average), so set your expectations and consider how you will manage your energy and emotions throughout the process.

• Make sure you keep a simple diary of your progress and conversations so you can refer back to it. At the end of the process, you can always ask that the increase is backdated to the start of the process.

_____

_____

_____

_____

_____

6. Be brave when it counts.

- Once you have walked through your case with your manager and it's time to talk turkey, you have two choices: put your preferred world number on the table or put no figure on the table.

- Whichever path you choose, you need to end with 'So, what are your thoughts?' then say nothing for as long as you can – about 45 seconds should do it. Shhhhh! They are the manager, let them lead.

PREPARE

☐ GAVE IT A GO

Actions for next time

Notes

☐ GOT IT

Stage 3:
LET'S GET STARTED –
TIME TO ENGAGE

ENGAGE

Now the real fun begins! It's time to go out and ENGAGE in a negotiation. If you've worked through the activities to date this shouldn't fill you with too much dread. Yes, you are likely to be anxious – but you can do it!

The objective is to get you more comfortable and more confident, and the best way to do that is through experience.

During the engagement phase, there are many things that may come up for you that will test your mettle. But as your confidence grows, you will be able to deal with anything that comes up for you.

Start seeing it as a game

Engagement Strategies

1. At the heart of removing the emotions and stress from all negotiations is to start seeing it as a game. If you've made it this far you should feel ready to **PLAY THE GAM**E.

2. Everyone needs ways to **MANAGE NERVES** so they aren't overwhelmed during negotiations.

3. One of your biggest assets is your ability to **READ THE PLAY**. These skills rely on your natural instincts and abilities. So start backing yourself and listening to your instincts to help you get the most out of each negotiation, or to know when to get out of there.

4. It can feel like an emotional rollercoaster so it's important to **MANAGE YOUR EMOTIONS** throughout the process. It may be a block that is easier to remove than you think. If negotiations didn't

ENGAGE

stir up strong emotions in you, you could start to enjoy them and approach them with a positive mindset.

5. However, there may be difficulties: the higher the stakes, the more likely you will need to know how to **DEAL WITH CHALLENGES**.

In this section, you will undertake in a series of activities to build your skills and confidence as you engage in more negotiations.

This may be daunting at first, and you may want to close this book right now – but please don't! You've done a lot of leg work up to this point, so give a couple of the activities a go and note how you feel and how your confidence is growing.

Negotiating is a series of choices

Remember my golden rule: negotiating is a series of choices, and you can get off the bus any time you are feeling too uncomfortable. However, you must get on the bus to kick things off. Let's get on board!

Strategy: Play the game

The key to your success is to find ways to remove or manage the emotions and stress associated with negotiations. They will always be there, so it's about how you can quieten the voice inside your head. One way to do this is to start seeing negotiations as a game.

ENGAGE

It probably sounds odd, but by making a game of something you find stressful, you can remove a great deal of tension. You can also use this strategy to help you think about what's going on in the third person – removing yourself and your personal roadblocks from the situation.

This is another way of viewing negotiations as something you can opt in and out of as you wish. It's not unlike the bus analogy: you can stop the game whenever you want, but once you start to view negotiating as a game, you'll start to find the fun in playing it. Start enjoying yourself - laugh a little along the way - until you are really relishing it.

Now you've done all the groundwork and your confidence is building, it's time to get in the game.

ACTIVITIES: PLAY THE GAME

Don't ask, don't get	page 108
Fake it 'til you make it	page 110
Price beat not price match please	page 112
Push it	page 114

ENGAGE

Strategy: Nerves mean it matters

Everyone gets nervous – even Masters! If people say they don't get nervous from time to time, they're fibbing.

I never know if it's nervous excitement or nervous anxiety but, no matter which one, I take time to acknowledge how I'm feeling before I start any negotiation.

It's all part of the game. Certainly not one that we love, but it can be managed with some conscious effort. Keep perspective. Look up. Take a time-out. And breathe.

ACTIVITIES: NERVES MEAN IT MATTERS

Managing your nerves	page 116
Break it down	page 118
Slow down, no rush	page 120

Strategy: Read the play

Use all your senses to best position yourself in a negotiation. It's easy to focus too much on you and how you're feeling during these conversations, but the more you take time to look outwards and note what is going on for the other person, the easier things should become.

ENGAGE

Firstly, if you are not focused on yourself, then you will naturally become less nervous and more confident. And, secondly, this will help you to know if things are going well or not, so you can quickly turn things around or decide to step away from the game.

Let's take a moment to think about how the brain makes decisions.

In an article entitled 'Decision-Making', Susan Perry from the Society for Neuroscience explains decision making in layman's terms: "Our brains appear wired in ways that enable us, often unconsciously, to make the best decisions possible with the information we're given. In simplest terms, the process is organized like a court trial. Sights, sounds, and other sensory evidence are entered and registered in sensory circuits in the brain. Other brain cells act as the brain's 'jury', compiling and weighing each piece of evidence. When the accumulated evidence reaches a critical threshold, a judgment — a decision — is made."

ACTIVITIES: READ THE PLAY

Trust your gut	page 122
Body language	page 124
The wry smile	page 126

ENGAGE

Strategy: Manage your emotions

The pain most people associate with negotiating is a belief that it's going to be a fight. This is based on the idea that we only negotiate on things that matter, so they are bound to be an emotional minefield. I believe this is the single biggest reason why people do not like negotiating. And I think it's a falsely held belief.

Negotiations are not a place to make friends, nor are they places to make enemies. But, unfortunately, it can happen if emotions are not kept in check.

People can get a bit crazy when they are talking about money. There is a feeling that it's personal. But it's not!

Most Australians have grown up in a culture where money is not often discussed, so the first step is to accept that we have to talk about money. Until this becomes part of what we do as a culture, things may be a little uncomfortable. But it's OK!

As I mentioned in the beginning of this book, when money is involved, emotions typically (and naturally) follow closely behind. They will always be there, but you get to choose if they control the situation or if you are simply conscious of them and can manage them.

In the 2013 article 'Making Emotions Work for You in Negotiations' by Shirli Kopelman, professor at the University of Michigan's Ross School of Business, she says, "…in my two decades of research and work with thousands of executives, I've found that emotions shouldn't be

ENGAGE

managed or overcome. Rather, positive and negative emotions are valuable resources that you can use to your advantage.

"Positive and negative emotions are valuable resources that you can use to your advantage" Shirli Kopelman

"The key is to recognize during the negotiation what emotion you're feeling, then quickly evaluate whether it will help or hinder you, and without taking a break, intensify or decrease the feeling, or in some cases change the emotion altogether."

Next, we need to appreciate that as negotiations tend to take place over a considerable period of time, those involved will often get tired – this is likely to lead to frustration. It's important to be realistic and to be aware of your tolerance. Build in help as required.

The key to being a good negotiator is being able to find ways to avoid or to rectify difficult situations when emotions do get the better of you.

This series of activities will assist you with keeping your emotions in check, and ultimately make it easier for you to enjoy negotiating.

ENGAGE

ACTIVITIES: MANAGE YOUR EMOTIONS

Face your fears	page 128
FOMO tactics	page 130
Stop the backflips	page 132
Don't lose your head	page 134

Strategy: Managing challenges

Unfortunately, things sometimes run off the rails in a negotiation. We do everything possible to prevent this; however, when the stakes are high, it sometimes just happens. It certainly isn't intentional on anybody's part, but somehow focus gets lost and neither party really enjoys the process.

To be honest, it is very rare for things to run off the rails. You may leave a negotiation disappointed, but rarely does it end in a fight or an explosion.

Hopefully this book will help you never leave the negotiation table feeling disappointed again.

And, if a negotiation does go off the rails, you will know how to get things back on track. This is assuming that you don't want to walk away (refer to the section titled 'Fold 'em' if you do).

ENGAGE

For one-off deals or transactional exchanges such as buying a fridge, this is probably never going to happen. As I mentioned previously, you might walk away miffed, but it's unlikely to end in a tense exchange.

However, for deals where you will have an ongoing relationship with the other party, not being able to manage challenges could set you back for a long time if things are not managed or discussed in a mature fashion.

It's time to view challenges from a different perspective. Dr Nate Regier, author of *Beyond Drama*, discusses the roots of conflict: "At its most basic level, all conflict is, 'I'm not getting what I want', and there's nothing selfish about that, it's just a disconnect. So that conflict of energy has such incredible potential and if we can help take that conflict and turn it into something amazing, and something positive, then all that energy can be spent towards accomplishing wonderful things instead of what we call drama. Which is a misuse of the energy of conflict."

"Energy can be spent towards accomplishing wonderful things"

Dr Nate Regier

ENGAGE

So, a conflict doesn't have to be dramatic, but it can be if you are not comfortable removing emotions from the issues. This section should help you with some of the challenges you might face.

Things come up during a negotiation that you don't realise were important to you until they are potentially taken off the table. This might push your buttons, but in the words of Kerry Patterson in *Crucial Conversations: Tools for Talking When Stakes Are High*, the time has come to discuss, "What do I really want for myself? What do I really want for others? What do I really want for the relationship?" It's time to talk it through.

ACTIVITIES: MANAGING CHALLENGES

DON'T ASK, DON'T GET

STRATEGY	PLAY THE GAME
PROFILE	AVOIDER

ENGAGE

OVERVIEW

Sometimes, you can miss an opportunity simply by not asking for something. This can be so frustrating. You know that feeling you get when a friend has the exact same experience as you? Maybe you've both met someone you admire, but she comes back with that person's phone number. You ask 'how did you get that?!' and she simply replies: 'I just asked' – ahhhhhh, if only you knew it would be that easy. As the saying goes, if you don't ask, you don't get. So it's time to get used to asking.

ACTION

As an Avoider, you probably rarely ask for what you want. It's time to start speaking up for the things you want on a regular basis.

Start with the smallest of things. For example, after you've ordered your cappuccino and it arrives, ask the waitress for some extra cocoa on top. Look for opportunities to ask for what you want.

Practice this for all manner of things. Start noticing what you thought the other person would say or do when you asked for what you wanted. Then notice how they actually reacted. **You'll probably start to notice that most of what you are asking for is not that big a deal**.

Yes, you will come across some people who roll their eyes and make it feel like it's an inconvenience. Keep your observations broad and don't be put off by some upstart who probably shouldn't be working in the service industry.

The example above will help you find your voice that you can develop until you are comfortable to try the following activities:

1. When you are buying whitegoods or similar products, simply ask the salesperson if they are open to a discount for cash? They may

say no, to which you can easily say thank you, and move on to asking about payment. At least you opened the door to the conversation. But they may say yes! If they do, that's great. Now ask them, 'what's your best price?' I'm sure at this level you'll be happy with whatever they say, as long as it's less than the ticket price. So smile and say thanks! Job done.

2. Visit your local farmer's markets; they are a hotbed of people who love bartering and negotiating on price, so this is a great training ground with low risk of you diminishing your confidence. Ask your friendly fruit vendor 'how much?' for one banana. He may be used to people buying things in bulk, so he might be surprised by this question. Then ask him how much for three bananas. If he says it's $1 for one and $3 for three bananas tell him you'll give him $2 for the three bananas. In my experience, the vendor is highly likely to say yes, or counter offer at $2.50.

Don't overthink this, just throw the words out there and see if they catch on. Market vendors tend to love the thrill of haggling; you'll probably get a grin out of him to boot!

☐ *GAVE IT A GO*

Actions for next time

_____

_____

Notes

_____

_____

_____

_____

☐ *GOT IT*

FAKE IT 'TIL YOU MAKE IT

STRATEGY	PLAY THE GAME
PROFILE	DABBLER

ENGAGE

OVERVIEW

It's time to focus on your attitude, back yourself and step out with a different perspective.

ACTION

It's time to change the way you shop and where you shop.

1. Shop at stores that are open to negotiation on price

- Large or major retailers can offer the prices they do because they have negotiated a bulk-buy discount for themselves. Then, to make a profit, they put the biggest possible margin on each item. If you're not sure if they're open to negotiation, the simplest thing to do is to call them or ask them in store if they are open to discounts for cash.

2. When you are shopping in these stores:

- Start by asking them the price, then casually ask them if that's their best price.
- Then WAIT – give them 15 seconds to consider what you have asked them (watch your watch if need be).

3. They will typically say, 'we can probably do something':

- Then they will take you to the computer (to check their margin on that item).
- In my experience, they will always propose something cheaper, even if it's only a small amount.

4. The more confident you become:

- The more you will be able to push them a little harder on the price by simply saying 'is that REALLY the best you can do?'

5. Some other things you can throw in the mix are:

ENGAGE

- Tell them you're paying by cash and see if that makes a difference. Note: cash doesn't mean folding money, just not on credit.

- If they can't take any more off the price, ask them if they can throw anything else into the deal as a sweetener. For example, if you are buying a computer, perhaps they can throw in anti-virus software or a carry bag for free?

- Sometimes there really is no margin to play with and there's only so far you can push this approach. Remember, you are aiming for a fair and reasonable exchange – not to win at all costs.

☐ GAVE IT A GO

Actions for next time

_____

_____

_____

_____

Notes

_____

_____

_____

_____

_____

_____

_____

☐ GOT IT

PRICE BEAT NOT PRICE MATCH PLEASE

ENGAGE

STRATEGY	PLAY THE GAME
PROFILE	DABBLER

OVERVIEW

When you know there is room to flex, you should take advantage of it – on reasonable terms, not on the ones they have laid out.

ACTION

Lots of companies profess to price match (rather than price beat). I've always been a little perplexed by this; why would I bother going to the effort and expense of driving to that store if they're only willing to match, rather than beat, a price?

Your task here is to ask a business what their Price Beat policy is, even if they only profess to offer a Price Match policy. Give them a minute to consider this perspective; hopefully they will also see the futility of price matching and reconsider their price further. There's no harm in trying!

☐ GAVE IT A GO

Actions for next time

ENGAGE

Notes

☐ GOT IT

PUSH IT

STRATEGY	PLAY THE GAME
PROFILE	ADVENTURER

OVERVIEW

Push the other party a little to see how they react. It really helps if you are naturally, or happy to be, a little bit cheeky. The key here is to listen, reflect, decide what's appropriate, and then act.

ACTION

The key to pushing someone a little harder than they think they can be pushed, is to listen. People often speak a lot during a negotiation because they're nervous. This provides you with a fantastic opportunity to pick up on things.

I recently had series of dramatic events with my mum. She was waiting for several months to have surgery on her knee, when unfortunately she fell over and broke her arm – arghhhhh!

When I rang the surgeon's office to explore the chances of the operation still going ahead, the receptionist came back and said no, on the grounds that my mum would need the use of her arms for the recovery.

This was a devastating blow and one I was not looking forward to telling my mum; so, I took a moment to think through what the receptionist had said to me. I realised that my mum may not need her arm for recovery if she had a full-time carer during recovery (i.e. me, Daughter of the Year).

After much toing and froing and several chats with the surgeon, we were back on with the operation – woohoo! In reflection, this outcome was 100 per cent about taking a moment to really listen to the objection the other party had to my request.

Next time you find yourself across the table from someone who is rejecting your request, take some time to think back over the words they have shared. **What are they saying the real problem is?**

You may need to call a time-out to give your mind the space to think this through and replay what you have just heard. This will give you the time you need to come up with a suggested solution for discussion.

ENGAGE

A time-out will also help ensure that you don't miss any opportunities and that you don't push too hard, as you will be more focused on them, rather than on yourself.

Now that you've given this a go, think about what went well? What would you do differently next time?

☐ GAVE IT A GO

Actions for next time

_____

_____

_____

_____

Notes

_____

_____

_____

_____

_____

_____

_____

☐ GOT IT

MANAGING YOUR NERVES

STRATEGY   NERVES MEAN IT MATTERS

PROFILE   AVOIDER

OVERVIEW

Nerves are normal. They are a sign that this negotiation matters to you. But don't let them consume you.

ACTION

Here are five simple tips for managing your nerves:

- **Breathe**. Take six big, slow breaths in and out before you walk in. Make sure you are as comfortable as possible before you start a conversation that matters.

- **Worst-case scenario**. Think about what's at risk. What's the worst possible outcome from the discussion? Think through that for a moment. OK, now that you know the worst-possible outcome, revisit your plan, adjust it or work through it and stay aware of your anxiety levels.

- **Dress the part**. If you have a power suit or a pair of shoes that makes you feel super-confident, crack them out of the wardrobe. These will build your confidence from the get-go.

- **Go early**. Don't spend all day thinking about having this conversation. In Brian Tracy's book *Eat that Frog* he explains 'Principle 17: Do the Most Difficult Task First'. His premise is that the rest of your day will be easier because you've conquered the most difficult task first. It really works, so try it!

- **Keep perspective**. You're not asking for something outrageous, you are just having a conversation that you hope will end up with a fair and reasonable exchange. No big deal, so relax.

After all these years of negotiating, I still get nervous! I have asked many mentors if they do too, and most people say yes. But how you manage them is key, The more you are conscious of your nerves the easier they are to manage, for example for me, one of my 'tells' when I'm nervous is that I speak really fast. So to combat this I have to remember to breath – it's so simple, but extremely effective. It's important to take note of how you're feeling at various times during a negotiation – your nerves definitely fluctuate – sometimes they won't be there at all. As you become aware of how you are reacting you can take action as needed.

☐ GAVE IT A GO

Actions for next time

_____

_____

_____

_____

_____

Notes

_____

_____

_____

_____

_____

_____

_____

_____

_____

☐ GOT IT

BREAK IT DOWN

STRATEGY	NERVES MEAN IT MATTERS
PROFILE	DABBLER

ENGAGE

OVERVIEW

You have probably built this negotiation 'situation' up quite significantly in your mind. You may have put a great deal of pressure on yourself. Perhaps you are feeling the weight of that right now? It's time to dissect what you're really trying to achieve, by when – and create a staged approach.

ACTION

I will again refer to *Eat that Frog* by Brian Tracey for this one: 'Principle 12: Take it One Oil Barrel at a Time'. Most of us have a tendency to look only to the end goal or the outcome, but **it's important to focus on the milestones along the way** - that way you don't get side-tracked by only thinking about the bigger picture or end game. Consider which milestones should you focus on along the way? What's the next 'oil barrel' you need to get to?

Think about a personally important negotiation coming up and break it down into stages. **Start at the end-game, then work backwards through the stages**. What are the milestones? What do you want to achieve that will contribute to the ultimate goal? What are all the tasks you'll need to do along the way? Write a list, then put them in chronological order.

A simple example might be talking to colleague about their team helping out with a project you are leading. It is good to write down a what the end of the discussion would look like, what do you ideally want (how many people, for how long, and how much time per day you will need them for), what does success look like for the project, and what would your colleague gain from contributing this time and these resources? Start from there then keep writing, perhaps think about all their objections and all the things you and your team can do for them in return (if that's required).

Once you have this picture work backwards on what you need to do to make it happen. You may need to speak to a number of people to get approval to pull this off, so work that through and make a list of actions. Then get to it…

ENGAGE

As you approach the first stage try to focus on the outcome of that stage only – not the whole game. Once you reach the first stage, which could be as simple as setting up the meeting, congratulate yourself and look to the next task.

This will take discipline. You will need to keep reminding yourself that you have a staged approach. And you need to relax, be good to yourself, and breathe.

☐ *GAVE IT A GO*

Actions for next time
_____
_____
_____
_____
_____

Notes
_____
_____
_____
_____
_____
_____

☐ *GOT IT*

SLOW DOWN, NO RUSH

ENGAGE

STRATEGY	NERVES MEAN IT MATTERS
PROFILE	ADVENTURER

OVERVIEW

It's natural to want to wrap things up quickly, but if you rush into it, people will think you are a bit of a robot. Chit-chat is important. The calmer everyone is in these situations, the better the outcome. If you can set the scene early and not rush, you will be in a strong position to achieve a positive outcome.

ACTION

A wise manager once told me that I should **learn to hasten slowly**. It took a LONG time for me to understand what this meant and then to live by it, but now I do.

It really helps if you aren't in a hurry to wrap things up or to get to the point quickly. I am a very functional and practical person so I never really enjoy small talk. I think it's a waste of time. But I do love to learn about people, so I realised that starting a key meeting by talking about what people have been up to or what they did on the weekend isn't a waste of my time, it's interesting. AND it gives you an opportunity to really listen, ask questions and obtain an air of calm before getting into the meat of the discussion. Small talk essentially helps establish a personal, human connection with the other side. This is important because:

1. Negotiations are emotionally charged and it can help make the other side feel at ease; and

2. People make decisions based on how they feel, not just the facts, so taking the time to make this personal connection makes the other side more likely to understand your needs and puts you in a better position to receive a favourable outcome from them.

Based on what you know about the other person's style, decide if you want to lead the conversation or let them lead it. Consider things such as their position, cultural background, history of your relationship, how negotiations with this person have played out in the past, what the person likes/dislikes, age, gender? Do any of those matter or influence how you approach the negotiation?

ENGAGE

If they are leading, sit back and play the game until you have gauged the situation. Take time to consider your position and to centre yourself.

If you are leading, **don't rush into the heart of the conversation too quickly**. Shoot the breeze, talk about the weekend, then set the scene. Outline how you see the discussion going and reach agreement on the agenda for the meeting. This first step will help generate a positive and inclusive vibe in the room. Then you are off and into it.

☐ *GAVE IT A GO*

Actions for next time

_____

_____

_____

_____

Notes

_____

_____

_____

_____

_____

☐ *GOT IT*

TRUST YOUR GUT

STRATEGY   READ THE PLAY

PROFILE   AVOIDER

ENGAGE

OVERVIEW

I believe there is an extra sense within us that lets us know if things are right or wrong. Gut instinct is a strong indicator of how you should proceed. You need to listen to it and back it.

ACTION

There are times when your spidey-sense, gut instinct or voice in your head kicks in and tells you something isn't right. It's a feeling that overrides nerves, but it's often set to one side until later when you reflect on the situation and think to yourself, I knew something wasn't right.

Well, don't wait for that to happen during your reflection time. Practice being more aware of your feelings and how you are reacting to the situation. **If something doesn't feel right take your time to think about why that is**. Perhaps ask yourself a few exploratory questions: Why is it this? Or could it be that? How else can I shape it?

If this eases the discomfort, keep talking. If not, you might just need to choose to walk away from this particular negotiation.

I usually find the times I don't listen to the voice in my head or trust my instinct someone else has the same feeling but as things are going well, you don't want to be the one to say 'hey, I'm just feeling a bit funky about this – not sure what it is, but something's not quite right'. It's a brave thing to do, but it can also say you a tonne of pain later on. You may need to call a little time out to have a chat with your team or partner and just chat things. One thing I try to do in these situations is to be as removed as possible from the discussion – if my best friend came to me with this would I think it's a good deal?

☐ GAVE IT A GO

Actions for next time

ENGAGE

Notes

☐ GOT IT

BODY LANGUAGE

STRATEGY	READ THE PLAY
PROFILE	DABBLER

ENGAGE

OVERVIEW

Body language can guide you during key discussions. You just need to know what to look out for.

ACTION

In Allan and Barbara Pease's book The Definitive Book of Body Language, they state that "Most researchers now agree that words are used primarily for conveying information, while body language is used for negotiating interpersonal attitudes and, in some cases, is used as a substitute for verbal messages." Being aware of the other person's body language can assist you greatly.

Here are five body language signals to look out for as an indicator of how your negotiation is going.

1. The power of smiling

A genuine smile creates positive feelings and encourages trust. But, don't overdo it – you don't want to look weird. Remember to take a moment at the beginning to build trust and if things are amusing throughout the process, enjoy it, smile and laugh.

2. Eye contact

Ensure you are maintaining eye contact. This conveys openness, sincerity and trust. If either party stops the eye contact, this is a 'tell'. Take a moment to understand what's going on for them, ask them if they have a concern they want to share.

3. Keep an open posture

Research conducted by Allan and Barbara Pease shows that when volunteers listening to a lecture folded their arms, not only did they learn and retain 38 per cent less information than volunteers who maintained uncrossed arms, but they also had more critical opinions of the lecturer. You may not even realise you're doing this, so be aware of how you're sitting. Also, how the other party is sitting. Crossed arms could indicate they are not open to negotiation or discussion at this point in time so it might be better move on or to pause and re-convene at a later time if possible.

4. Facial expressions

Not many people have a fantastic or constant poker face, so keep an eye on their facial reactions when you speak. Conversely, you should mind your own reactions, so you aren't an open book. For me, I have 'default-sad face', I was born with it - so sometimes people can read me wrong, so I have to be mindful of this in negotiations so I am not misunderstood during the process.

5. Beware of crossed legs

Crossed legs indicate a person is mentally, emotionally and physically closed off — this means they are less likely to be flexible in a negotiation. In Gerard Nierenberg and Henry Calero's book How to Read a Person Like a Book they found that out of 2000 videotaped negotiations, there wasn't a single settlement made when one of the negotiators had their legs crossed.

As you become more aware of your own body language – and the other person's – you can ask curious questions to ensure each of you is more comfortable, and to help keep things on track. Their body language may even tell you how they are feeling, so you may want to call a time-out based on what you see.

☐ *GAVE IT A GO*

Actions for next time

_____

_____

Notes

_____

_____

☐ *GOT IT*

THE WRY SMILE

STRATEGY	READ THE PLAY
PROFILE	ADVENTURER

ENGAGE

OVERVIEW

There is a time in a negotiation when you know you've had a breakthrough with the other party. I call it 'The Wry Smile' – and I love it when I see it!

ACTION

You need to be patient and you need to sometimes be a little cheeky – but, most of all, **you need to be your most likeable self**.

I typically see the wry smile when I'm trying to get more of something or when I'm getting out of trouble. I think I may have perfected this as a tactic with my parents, trying to getting out of trouble.

Imagine you have run back to your car, knowing your parking ticket has expired. You happen to get back at the exact time the parking inspector is reading the expired parking ticket.

You note he hasn't written you a ticket yet, so there is a window of opportunity to convince them to let this one slide…

It's time to appeal to their human side. Think about how many people get mad at these guys every day – lots!

A few kind words, a plea and an apology (I'm sorry, I was catching up a friend and time slipped away, is it too late? Have you written it up yet? Please, please….), followed by a pause… wait, wait, wait… BANG! The wry smile appears! 'Woohoo, thank you, thank you, have a great day, I'm leaving now, bye!'

If that smile doesn't appear, at least you gave it a go and you might have brightened their day. Don't ask, don't get, right?

There are many opportunities to seek out the wry smile, so start looking for it. Remember, time is your friend in allowing the other party time to consider what you have put forward. When the moment arrives, you should see their face relax and you'll know you have a deal.

ENGAGE

☐ GAVE IT A GO

Actions for next time

_____

_____

_____

_____

_____

_____

Notes

_____

_____

_____

_____

_____

_____

_____

_____

_____

_____

☐ GOT IT

FACE YOUR FEARS

STRATEGY	MANAGE YOUR EMOTIONS
PROFILE	AVOIDER

OVERVIEW

The greatest handbrake for most Avoiders is fear. It's time to look fear in the face and understand what you are really afraid of.

ACTION

It is often said that **many people are better at negotiating on behalf of others than for themselves**, and this is a great starting point to help you face your fears.

For me, negotiating on behalf of someone else feels like I'm helping someone, doing something good. In contrast, for some people negotiating for themselves can feel greedy or bad.

Think about the last time you helped someone get something they wanted. Perhaps you secured a pay rise for a staff member?

If this activity didn't grip you with fear, then there is a lesson in it to help you when negotiating for yourself.

Think back over that activity and note down anything you did that could help you. Then consider the wise words of Spencer Johnson in *Who Moved my Cheese*: "Now, go and do what you did for someone else – for yourself!"

☐ GAVE IT A GO

Actions for next time

_____

_____

_____

_____

_____

_____

ENGAGE

Notes

_____

_____

_____

_____

_____

_____

_____

_____

_____

_____

_____

_____

_____

_____

_____

_____

☐ GOT IT

FOMO TACTICS

STRATEGY	MANAGE YOUR EMOTIONS
PROFILE	DABBLER

OVERVIEW

Salespeople are highly trained individuals and some of them are excellent at getting you to part with your cash on things you may not really want. Then, before you know it, you end up with buyer's remorse.

Sales tactics are frequently based on fear. These strategies centre on fostering anxiety through scarcity. However, it's easy to detect these once you start looking for them.

FOMO, Fear Of Missing Out, is one of the most successful tactics as it is often wrapped up in a simple sales message.

1. 'For a limited time only'

Ever noticed how sales just keep on going and going? More like an 'unlimited time only'! Don't be fooled, do your 'background check', don't rush in.

2. 'This is a limited edition'

Originally created by the fashion industry, exclusivity has a cachet like no other. Ask yourself if this item is really unique, or simply an ordinary item with a logo slapped on it?

3. 'Only five remaining'

A countdown can help drive sales, but sadly it's often untruthful. It's easy to feel panicked and pressured to buy something if you think it's one of the last few. Ask store staff if there are really only five left, or ring around other stores and check for yourself.

4. 'Major sales sprints'

Events such as the Boxing Day and Black Friday sales have created a fantastic sales event, but realistically aren't these stores just marking up the prices leading into these sales so you feel like you are getting a bargain during the sale? Wait for the sale, if you can.

5. 'This is why you need it'

How salespeople explain why you need something is a good indicator of their integrity. They will often focus on what you are missing out on in your life by not having this item. Listen to how they describe the need. Be critical; if it feels like spin, it probably is!

6. A major FOMO tactic can happen when you are looking at cars.

The salesperson is likely to suggest they write up a 'no obligation' quote for you. Once that is done, if you happen to suggest you'll come back tomorrow to finish the deal, the salesperson is likely to say something like, "I probably won't be able to make this same offer to you tomorrow." As you've invested so much time in getting the quote written up, you might be tempted to just sign up and get it done. DON'T fall for it! The reality is there is no scarcity with buying your average car, you can walk down the road tomorrow and buy one next door that looks pretty much the same, and you could probably use that quote to help you get a better deal (that's really what the salesperson is afraid of).

ACTION

Being aware of these tactics makes it easier to say no to them.

In Dr Robert Cialdini's book Influence he outlines the many ways to say 'no'. With regard to scarcity, his advice is: "Should we find ourselves beset by scarcity pressures in a compliance situation, then, our best response would occur in a two-stage sequence. As soon as we feel the tide of emotional arousal that flows from scarcity influences, we should use that rise in arousal as a signal to stop short. Panicky, feverish reactions have no place in wise compliance decisions. We need to calm ourselves and regain a rational perspective. Once that is done, we can move to the second stage by asking ourselves why we want the item under consideration. If the answer is that we want it primarily for the purpose of owning it, then we should use its availability to help gauge how much we want to spend for it. However, if the answer is that we want it primarily for its function (that is, we want something good to drive, drink, eat, etc.), then we must remember that the item under consideration will function equally well whether scarce or plentiful. Quite simply, we need to recall that the scarce cookies didn't taste any better."

☐ *GOT IT*

STOP THE BACKFLIPS

STRATEGY	MANAGE YOUR EMOTIONS
PROFILE	DABBLER

ENGAGE

OVERVIEW

You've done all your preparation, you're ready to go, you've set up the conversation – then you get in there and you turn to jelly. You backflip, and you get outta there as quickly as possible. No more! It's time to be brave and back yourself.

ACTION

It's important to manage your emotions when you walk into the lion's den. The backflip often occurs when the subject is personal, perhaps when discussing your pay rise.

You may have it all mapped out in your head, you've done all your prep work, but when you get into the discussion you find yourself agreeing to the first offer they put across the table!

The conversation may go a little like this:

YOU: *My position is X.*

Them: *NO.*

YOU: *Okay then, my position is X-1.*

OR

Them: *We're offering you $xx.*

YOU: *I was hoping for $xx+1.*

Them: *That's all we can do.*

YOU: *Okay.*

The next minute you walk out dazed and confused, and wondering where all your pre-meeting bravado went.

Chances are you forgot to dissociate yourself with the outcome. Perhaps you didn't anticipate how the conversation would go. Or your fear overcame you and you became a little mouse.

ENGAGE

If this happens, you have to dust yourself off and re-engage – as quickly as possible. When you feel the fear rising, do all you can to ignore it.

Ride the wave of the conversation, take your time and keep it as much at arm's length as possible. Pretend you are negotiating on someone else's behalf. But don't speak too much. Let your manager manage the situation. It's up to you to focus on how you manage yourself. What you anticipate will happen versus what actually happens is often very different, so it is vital that you stay cool and don't backflip - **instead of saying ok, say "that doesn't feel fair to me, can we talk about it?"**

☐ GAVE IT A GO

Actions for next time

_____

_____

_____

Notes

_____

_____

_____

_____

_____

☐ GOT IT

DON'T LOSE YOUR HEAD

ENGAGE

STRATEGY   MANAGE YOUR EMOTIONS

PROFILE   ADVENTURER

OVERVIEW

It can happen: unfortunately you can sometimes lose your head in a negotiation by letting yourself succumb to the frustrations involved. It's not good, but it's not unusual – and you can recover.

ACTION

In order to manage your emotions, you should acknowledge their existence. Take a moment to confirm what you are experiencing. Shirli Kopelman at the University of Michigan Ross School of Business says: "The key is to recognise during the negotiation what emotion you're feeling, then quickly evaluate whether it will help or hinder you, and without taking a break, intensify or decrease the feeling, or in some cases change the emotion altogether."

Shirli's point is a simple yet complicated one; if you are conscious of what's going on for you, the chain of events she has noted will naturally follow.

As has been mentioned throughout this book, some negotiations take a long time, so you can get a little frustrated. The reality is that you are sometimes dealing with people who aren't good negotiators – this can make them frustrating to deal with.

You may be working on a deal that is taking longer than you think it should be. It can be difficult to stay tolerant if you think the other party is dragging their feet for no good reason.

Combine this with your desire to close the deal with the best outcome for you and all of this can lead to some tense moments.

Often, when things get tense, we try to talk our way through the situation. For some people, this can accidentally become a debate.

Emotions can start to get frayed when the stakes are high. And these are times when you really need to hold your cards close and your mouth shut.

ENGAGE

When you feel your cheeks start to burn, you're in it! It's time to take a moment – sssssSSSSSSHHHHH. It doesn't matter if you are mid-sentence, just **stop talking and call things to a halt**.

☐ GAVE IT A GO

Actions for next time

_____
_____
_____
_____
_____
_____

Notes

_____
_____
_____
_____
_____
_____
_____

☐ GOT IT

TAKE THE HEAT OUT

STRATEGY	MANAGING CHALLENGES
PROFILE	DABBLER

ENGAGE

OVERVIEW

Once things escalate, it's important to take the heat out of a situation as quickly as possible.

ACTION

The first step is to take time out, walk away, get outside and look up for some perspective.

While you are out there, consider if you want to walk away or continue the negotiation.

Don't leave it too long; once time starts to drag, the chances are that a deal either won't be done or poor decisions will be made.

Come back together, sit down and confirm whether or not both parties want to continue discussions. If so, it's important to clear the air and agree you want to listen again to their side of the story, and they to yours.

Then talk through the challenges from each side's perspective.

If necessary, let each team discuss their thoughts and opinions and suggested way forward without the other team commenting or responding. The hope is that if each team is listening to the other, the conversation that follows should be productive and positive.

☐ GAVE IT A GO

Actions for next time

_____

_____

_____

_____

_____

_____

ENGAGE

Notes

_____

_____

_____

_____

_____

_____

_____

_____

_____

_____

_____

_____

_____

_____

☐ GOT IT

IT'S NOT PERSONAL

STRATEGY	MANAGING CHALLENGES
PROFILE	DABBLER

OVERVIEW

It's important to be specific in your choice of words and language when you negotiate. This is particularly important when you're dealing with people you'll be interacting with on an ongoing basis.

ACTION

It's important to be mindful that nothing in this situation is personal – it's business. In fact, you should specifically aim to depersonalise a negotiation.

Depersonalise the conversation as much as possible by choosing specific language when describing your position. It takes practice, but it makes a major difference.

Consider a particularly sensitive subject, such as negotiating your salary with your manager. You need to depersonalise your vocabulary as much as you can.

1. Replace 'you' with 'the company'. It's not your manager that decides the rules, it's the company. You want your manager to be your advocate so it's important you appreciate their position. When you're saying 'you haven't done this or that' it really is personal and it may put them on the back foot.

2. Next, it's important to swap 'me' with 'someone in my position'. You are asking for a pay rise because someone in your position, being asked to put in the hours, manage the staff, or deliver on certain KPIs would expect to be remunerated in the way you are suggesting. Your pay grade is not a privilege, it is an exchange of value (of your time for effort).

3. Finally, consider replacing 'I believe' with 'a reasonable person would think/do/act' in this situation. This simple twist will reduce the risk the other person feels you are blaming them.

Your goal is to separate the people from the problem; to remove the personal passion from the conversation.

This is one of the most effective methods of defusing a tense situation, but also a very difficult habit to get into – so practice it today.

ENGAGE

☐ GAVE IT A GO

Actions for next time

_____

_____

_____

_____

_____

Notes

_____

_____

_____

_____

_____

_____

_____

_____

_____

☐ GOT IT

CALL IT

STRATEGY	MANAGING CHALLENGES
PROFILE	ADVENTURER

ENGAGE

OVERVIEW

If you screw up, don't be too proud to apologise.

ACTION

It's rare that people mean to push too hard, but if you feel you have, step back and own up to it.

If you are on your way back from the bathroom, or if you wake up the day after a negotiation and think to yourself, 'I may have pushed a little too hard', tell the other person. Explain what your point was so they know you weren't just being an assh*le. With a clear head, you can clarify your position and re-engage in the discussion.

I was recently in a meeting where a woman was explaining that she'd saved her client hundreds of thousands of dollars with the work she had delivered. Despite this, her client had told her he felt her price was too high when he received the invoice. While we were talking it through, I suggested that there were likely two reasons why he felt her invoice was unreasonable:

1. She hadn't articulated the value in her report and subsequent invoice; hence, he was taken aback by her fee, OR

2. He was just tight.

We talked it through as a group and she seemed a little less distressed by the scenario; but it was nagging at me so I had a little break.

When I got back from the bathroom I made a point of apologising to the woman in front of the whole group. I don't know her well, and I may have been pushing her too hard with my synopsis of the situation.

I reiterated my point, which was that she shouldn't beat herself up too much by her client's response. But nor should she reduce her fee just because he was surprised by the invoice. However, I probably came across a little too direct with my displeasure of this injustice that happened to her (not me).

ENGAGE

Fairness is one of my core values and so I saw a little bit of red in this situation.

I did have the best of intentions, but this got lost by my disdain for this person's lack of fairness. Therefore, it was important for her to know that my point was about his injustice, not that she had got it wrong by not clarifying the scope of work.

If you feel you've overstepped the mark, do the right thing and apologise.

☐ *GAVE IT A GO*

Actions for next time

_____

_____

_____

_____

Notes

_____

_____

_____

_____

_____

☐ *GOT IT*

WEAR A DIFFERENT HAT

STRATEGY	**MANAGING CHALLENGES**
PROFILE	**ADVENTURER**

ENGAGE

OVERVIEW

We can sometimes create additional pressure in a negotiation by anticipating what might happen. This can influence your experience – in both positive and negative ways.

ACTION

Predominantly, you'll be entering into negotiations with an open mind. However, this may be hard to do if you have history or baggage from having dealt with the other party before, especially if it went awry.

Don't fall into the trap of anticipating how the other person may act or react. You may be wrong. People can be surprising, so pre-empting outcomes can be dangerous.

If things do stagnate because you're facing a similar situation to one you have experienced in the past with this same party, perhaps take a leaf from the wonderful genius of Dr Edward De Bono with his *Six Thinking Hats*. This is a framework to help people think clearly and thoroughly by directing their thinking attention in one direction at a time

- White hat – facts
- Green hat – creativity
- Yellow hat – benefits
- Black hat– cautions
- Red hat – feelings
- Blue hat - process

In very basic terms, you 'pick up' a hat and think about the problem or situation from only that viewpoint. The end result is that you get to see the same problem from different points of view.

This activity can help you **see things from the other side**.

I wouldn't suggest doing this as part of the negotiation process; it's more something your team could do in between catch-ups with the other party. It should help you come back with some alternate solutions or strategies.

ENGAGE

☐ GAVE IT A GO

Actions for next time

_____

_____

_____

_____

_____

Notes

_____

_____

_____

_____

_____

_____

☐ GOT IT

GIVE THEM AN OUT

STRATEGY	MANAGING CHALLENGES
PROFILE	ADVENTURER

ENGAGE

OVERVIEW

As a negotiation progresses, especially in more complicated deals, it's important to think a couple of steps ahead.

ACTION

You will have mapped out a game plan before you start, and you'll be thinking things through on the fly. Both parties will have the objective of avoiding or managing a challenging point in a negotiation.

One way to keep things objective is to read the play from the other side. **Think about things from the other side's perspective and consider their options**. If you suggest that they do something, or give you something, what might they say or do in response?

Once you have the options thought through, you can ensure you give them a way to back out (without losing face) as part of your suggestion.

A fabulous example of this is by an amazing businesswoman, with fantastic negotiation skills: Taylor Swift. When it was announced that Apple Music would launch on June 30 2015 and they would not pay artists for songs streamed during a free three-month trial period for new subscribers, Taylor let it be known that this was not OK.

But she gave them a huge opportunity to back out without losing face when she said via Tumblr: "It's not too late to change this policy and change the minds of those in the music industry who will be deeply and gravely affected by this."

This situation could have blown up into a serious, ongoing and very public argument with two music industry behemoths, but thanks to this one post, Apple took up the invitation to change the conversation and decided to pay artists during their free trial.

With Tay Tay as your guide, consider ways to aid your partner in negotiation with this mindset. It's not about being smug or righteous, it's about keeping the options open and simple.

ENGAGE

☐ GAVE IT A GO

Actions for next time

_____

_____

_____

_____

_____

Notes

_____

_____

_____

_____

_____

_____

_____

_____

☐ GOT IT

A NEUTRAL ADVISOR

STRATEGY	**MANAGING CHALLENGES**
PROFILE	**ADVENTURER**

OVERVIEW

There are times when you may reach an impasse. A time when you aren't able to find a way forward as a collective. This is when a third party can help. Their role is to clarify each party's position or to reframe the conversation, while not undermining the lead teams.

ACTION

If you realise you have reached an impasse it is highly recommended that you softly introduce the idea of an external person to help solve the problem. Simply suggesting that some fresh perspective or a new set of eyes/ears to talk things through might help the situation. There is no need to go like a bull at a gate making things dramatic, the simple truth is that you have talked it through a number of times and if you can't solve this there is no deal, so it's prudent to **get some independent help**.

Each party needs to agree who this 'mediator' is, and this person would typically be someone more senior than those in the room, someone with decision-making capabilities.

It doesn't mean you're at each other's throats, it is simply a co-ordinated approach with the sole focus of resolving a particular issue.

Ideally, this advisor remains in the mix until the time the matter is resolved.

☐ GAVE IT A GO

Actions for next time

_____

_____

_____

_____

_____

_____

ENGAGE

Notes

_____

_____

_____

_____

_____

_____

_____

_____

_____

_____

_____

_____

_____

_____

☐ GOT IT

Stage 4:
THE END IS NIGH –
IT'S TIME TO CLOSE

CLOSE

Not everyone on the selling side is a good closer. Things may feel ambiguous or be left unresolved, so it's good for you to learn how to close. This is where the rubber really hits the road and, if you shy away from leading the close, you can miss out or be left frustrated with yourself for not taking an opportunity.

This section will aid you in the art of closing: from talking about money through to using time as a key tactic. It will also give you clarity to know when and how to walk away if you don't want to make a deal.

Closing Strategies

1. **Time is your friend**
2. **Show me the money**
3. **Know when to fold 'em**

Strategy: Time is your friend

Time is a fantastic tool in closing a deal.

> "Make use of time,
> let not advantage slip."
> William Shakespeare

CLOSE

When things get tough, or you are feeling confused in a negotiation, it's important to buy yourself some time. Salespeople are trained to create situations where you don't notice the pressure building. They don't like it when you're aware of the power of time.

ACTIVITIES: TIME IS YOUR FRIEND

Time's best friend	page 152
Types of time-out	page 154
Time of year, month, day	page 156

Strategy: Show me the money

The time has come, you knew it was going to happen at some point, you can't avoid it any longer... it's time to discuss money. Take a deep breath and let's get into it...

ACTIVITIES: SHOW ME THE MONEY

Rip the band-aid	page 158
Don't negotiate with yourself	page 160
Don't go too far	page 162

CLOSE

Strategy: Know when to fold 'em

`Some deals just can't be done, specifically when your opinions of the value of an item or service does not meet in the middle. Remember, it's not personal. This is a financial transaction, so you need to follow the advice of the great Kenny Rogers and "know when to fold 'em".

ACTIVITIES: KNOW WHEN TO FOLD 'EM

Just say 'No thanks'	page 164
Not good enough	page 166
Value misalignment	page 168

> "Know when to walk away, know when to run."
>
> Kenny Rogers

Stage 4: It's time to close

TIME'S BEST FRIEND

CLOSE

STRATEGY	TIME IS YOUR FRIEND
PROFILE	AVOIDER

OVERVIEW

Silence is a very good friend of time. Thirty seconds is an excruciating amount of silence, but it will deliver an outcome.

ACTION

When you make an offer, it's time to wait. DO NOT say anything for thirty seconds. DO NOT do anything. Even though your heart will be racing like mad, just play it cool. Watch your watch if necessary, but DO NOT speak.

This is time for the other party to consider what you have offered. It's their opportunity to decide if they are happy with what you have suggested, or if they are going to make a counter offer.

There are a number of possible next steps:

- If they say that's just too low, you should invite them to make you a counter offer.
- If they make a counter offer, great, just talk it through and finalise the deal.
- Or, you will see the wry smile appear. Happy days, deal done.

☐ GAVE IT A GO

Actions for next time

_____

_____

_____

_____

_____

_____

CLOSE

Notes

_____

_____

_____

_____

_____

_____

_____

_____

_____

_____

_____

_____

_____

_____

☐ *GOT IT*

TYPES OF TIME-OUT

STRATEGY	TIME IS YOUR FRIEND
PROFILE	DABBLER

(CLOSE)

OVERVIEW

If you feel like you're struggling for perspective in a negotiation, it's important to call a time-out.

ACTION

There are two types of time out that I find effective:

1. 'Blow the whistle' time-out

When it feels that you aren't making any progress, or you're struggling for perspective, or if you feel you are being pressured – it's time for a 'blow the whistle' time-out.

The time-out doesn't have to be long – thirty minutes might do, depending on the situation and reason for the time-out. Its purposes are to:

- let you recap on where things are at, relative to where you wanted or envisaged them to be at this stage
- defuse a tense moment
- give you a chance to chat with someone else about where to next, or to make a decision on a particular point
- give you a chance to think clearly, step out into the light and get a little perspective.

Once you return, you should feel a renewed energy for the discussion, and be experiencing less stress.

2. Toilet time-out

If you don't feel you can call a prolonged time-out, take a mini time-out: ask for a toilet break. I have no idea why this works, but for me it does – without fail. If I'm struggling to find perspective, I give my brain a little break and some breathing space: fresh air, five minutes and clean hands.

It can open up a whole new perspective and remind you of what's important. You can then step back into the discussion and continue with a renewed focus.

CLOSE

☐ GAVE IT A GO

Actions for next time

_____

_____

_____

_____

_____

_____

_____

Notes

_____

_____

_____

_____

_____

_____

_____

_____

_____

☐ GOT IT

TIME OF YEAR, MONTH, DAY

CLOSE

STRATEGY	TIME IS YOUR FRIEND
PROFILE	ADVENTURER

OVERVIEW

The time of day, the day of the month and the time of year can heavily influence your success.

ACTION

The particular day and time that you choose to have a key discussion can significantly influence the outcome of your negotiation.

Here are some timing issues to consider:

1. Time of year

- There are key times in all sales cycles that can be great for you to get a good deal. Think about times when sales staff are motivated by a deadline to meet a target. End of the month, end of the quarter, end of the financial year, for example.

2. Which day is best

- There are always optimal days in a business to have a negotiation. Mondays and Fridays are typically 'no-go', as these tend to be the busiest days. Make sure you pick the right day, based on your environment.
- When going to a retail store to negotiate, pick a day where there's likely to be less people. That way, the salesperson can be more open without risk of other customers jumping onto your negotiating bandwagon.

3. Time of day

- 'No problems before nine o'clock'. No-one wants to 'Eat Your Frog' – as author Brian Tracy would put it – for breakfast. Make sure you're presenting solutions if you're negotiating at this time of day.
- Book a typically clear time in the other party's diary so they can focus on your issue or request.
- Use the time of day to your advantage when you enter a high pressure sales environment. Visit a car dealership just after lunch so you have an excuse for a time-out – tell them you need to eat first.

People have said I am a little extreme, but if you want to put all of the above together, feel free to consider the way I go about buying a car:

CLOSE

- I aim for a time of year near the end of a sales cycle: end of month, end of financial year, end of 'plate' period. The sales team will be primed and ready to do a deal. You will typically have access to a senior decision maker onsite too, so they can approve a great deal without fuss.
- Ideally, I look to purchase a car on a Sunday on a slow sales weekend. One when it's been raining is best. The salespeople won't have too many people in the showroom, and are therefore able to openly discuss a good deal. And if they haven't hit their sales target due to the weather, they will more open to cutting a good deal.
- Finally, I arrive after lunch so I have an excuse to call a 'blow the whistle' time-out if they put too much pressure on me to close a deal that I'm not entirely comfortable with.

Okay, it is a rarity for all of these timings to align, but you get the idea: you have a much greater chance of securing a good deal if you think first about when you're going to negotiate.

A study by drivingsales.com found that **59% of American consumers hate negotiating car prices**. You don't have to hate it anymore!

☐ *GAVE IT A GO*

Actions for next time:

_____

_____

Notes

_____

_____

_____

☐ *GOT IT*

RIP THE BAND-AID

CLOSE

STRATEGY	SHOW ME THE MONEY
PROFILE	AVOIDER

OVERVIEW

That tension in the pit of your stomach will be at its most intense right now. But as soon as you rip off the Band-Aid it will loosen almost immediately.

ACTION

It's time to make the offer. Walk up to the salesperson – with all of your preparation top of mind – and the conversation might go a little like this:

THEM: Hi! How can I help you today? (Great start)

YOU: I'm looking for a xxxxx.

Here's where you use what you've learnt in all the activities in the 'It's Time to ENGAGE' section.

YOU: *And how much is this one?*

THEM: *$500*

YOU: *Is that your best price?*

THEM: *I'll see what I can do, let's go to the computer/desk/ equivalent…..*

THEM: *How about $480*

OPTION A You: *Great, thanks! Where do I pay?*

OPTION B You: *Is that anything more you can do (with a smile)?*

WOOHOO! YOU DID IT! WELL DONE. It's as easy as that…

☐ GAVE IT A GO

Actions for next time

CLOSE

Notes

☐ *GOT IT*

DON'T NEGOTIATE WITH YOURSELF

CLOSE

STRATEGY	SHOW ME THE MONEY
PROFILE	DABBLER

OVERVIEW

It's easy to get excited during a negotiation. If you really want something, and you're close to closing the deal, you might feel butterflies in your stomach. This is the key time to be careful. Don't let your heart rule your head until the deal is done. Stick to your game plan.

ACTION

When you get excited you risk doing the other party's job for them. In your head you're anticipating their position or their response to your offer. That can be a good thing; it means you're ready for the next part of the conversation. However, in your excitement, you may jump in and make a counter-offer before they even say anything. You might find yourself negotiating with yourself!

For example, if you're looking at buying a drum kit you might say to the seller you'll offer them $700, but before they even speak, you've read their negative facial reaction and you say, 'OK, how about $750?' You just negotiated with yourself and gave away $50 that you didn't need to.

Just wait, give them time to process your (lower) offer, watch your watch, and breathe. Excitement regularly leads you to speaking too much – and the more you talk, the more you give away. Not only that, the more you're talking, the less you are listening (which is really how we learn).

Don't make the arguments for them or make concessions that they haven't even requested. Don't move unless the other side makes a counter-offer or offers new information that warrants a concession.

Another quick tactic if you tend to get excited is to live by a 24-hour 'cooling off' period – simply don't make decisions that lock you in without 24 hours to sleep on it, and think over the impact of this purchase.

☐ GAVE IT A GO

Actions for next time
_____
_____
_____
_____
_____
_____

Notes
_____
_____
_____
_____
_____
_____
_____
_____
_____

☐ GOT IT

DON'T GO TOO FAR

CLOSE

STRATEGY   SHOW ME THE MONEY

PROFILE   ADVENTURER

OVERVIEW

We all want a good deal, but remember we are aiming for a good negotiation. It's not purely about you getting the best deal.

ACTION

The close can be a tough time to stay on track. Sometimes you can forget it's about both parties, and you might push a little too hard. Don't hold back from asking for a good deal, but **make sure you aren't playing hardball**. This is really important when bartering in third-world countries.

I have a beautiful set of soap stone carvings from Africa that a friend gave me years ago. The sad thing about them is that I was there when he negotiated with the seller. My friend was pushing really hard to get the price down (and down and down) – to the point where I was uncomfortable. To me, it was obvious that the seller wasn't having a good time; he needed the money and I felt my friend was exploiting that. I had to walk away, but he stayed and closed the sale.

Back then I was a Dabbler, so the whole situation made me very uncomfortable. But even then it played on my mind for a long time afterwards. It took me a while to feel that I could accept the gift, because it upset me to think about that man being ripped off.

What I learnt from that particular scenario was the power of a smile and its role in knowing when you're pushing too hard. Stay aware of the other party during the exchange and close the deal when you feel it's fair, not necessarily when you've got yourself a great deal.

[ ] GAVE IT A GO

Actions for next time

CLOSE

Notes

☐ GOT IT

JUST SAY 'NO THANKS'

STRATEGY	KNOW WHEN TO FOLD 'EM
PROFILE	AVOIDER

CLOSE

OVERVIEW

Don't get burdened with buyer's remorse because you felt you had to buy something out of obligation or because of FOMO; simply say 'no thanks'.

ACTION

Asking someone the price doesn't mean you are entering into a negotiation. But when you aren't confident, a savvy salesperson can sometimes pull you into this web.

Without noticing, you are all of a sudden in a discussion about price and the sales pitch is becoming all the more convincing.

Next minute, you get a flash of perspective and realise you don't need this particular thing or you don't see the value in it at the price quoted.

It's time to take a deep breath and just say 'thank you for your time, I'll think it over and come back'.

You've probably used this line in clothing stores many times. Just do the same thing and walk away. Buy yourself a wine and pat yourself on the back – job well done.

If you don't, you risk ending up with something that you don't want or need and it is highly unlikely that, as an Avoider, you will ever return it.

☐ GAVE IT A GO

Actions for next time

_____

_____

_____

_____

_____

_____

CLOSE

Notes

_____

_____

_____

_____

_____

_____

_____

_____

_____

_____

_____

_____

_____

_____

_____

_____

☐ GOT IT

NOT GOOD ENOUGH

STRATEGY   KNOW WHEN TO FOLD 'EM

PROFILE   DABBLER

OVERVIEW

It can be hard to walk away from a deal, but if you aren't enjoying the process, save your time and walk away.

ACTION

We often buy from people or stores we like, and this could be feeding into your overall desire for a certain item. As long as you can get this item from somewhere or someone else, you can FOLD 'EM based on how much you are enjoying the process of negotiating with this person. Remember, salespeople are often on commission, so do you really want to hand over your hard-earned cash to someone you don't particularly like?

There is an urban myth that explains this situation to a T: a guy walks into the showroom of a trucking company, Brand X. He's wearing stubbies and thongs and looks a bit scruffy. He asks the salesman about the prime mover and when it comes to the question of how much, the somewhat agitated salesman tells him, 'It's more than you can afford, mate'. The guy says, 'Cheers, mate' and leaves.

He heads to another trucking company, Brand Y, and upon arrival the salesperson greets him, asks questions and shows him the prime movers.

On the way home from buying 15 trucks worth about $18 million, the guy stops by Brand X and asks to speak to the earlier salesman's manager, where he tells him the 'good news': that his smug employee just cost him an $18M sale!

The lesson here is, **if you're not enjoying it, it's best to walk away** swiftly, without game playing, without a big fuss. You simply need to explain that it doesn't work for you, thank them for their time and leave.

☐ *GAVE IT A GO*

CLOSE

Actions for next time

_____

_____

_____

_____

_____

_____

Notes

_____

_____

_____

_____

_____

_____

_____

_____

_____

_____

_____

_____

☐ *GOT IT*

VALUE MISALIGNMENT

STRATEGY	KNOW WHEN TO FOLD 'EM
PROFILE	ADVENTURER

CLOSE

OVERVIEW

It can be hard to walk away from a deal, but if your valuations don't align, protect your wallet and walk away.

ACTION

Back to my time in Africa, I was in Malawi and really wanted a Malawi Chair. Each chair is unique, and if you've ever been to Malawi, you probably have one.

As I walked around the markets, I asked various vendors questions about how they made the chairs and the amount of effort that went into each one. I asked another how much they typically cost. And I asked our guide the average salary in Malawi.

So, before I entered the negotiation I spent some time calculating in my head how many hours/days had been invested in creating this spectacular piece that I had my heart set on.

Next, I calculated an approximate hourly rate (based on the exchange rate), then I added a 'tourist tax' (an expectation that tourists will pay more than a local). Then I felt I was all set, so I offered a little less than I was prepared to pay, knowing he would push me up.

Unfortunately for me, and the craftsman, after about 20 minutes of haggling we were still poles apart in our valuations so I HAD to walk away. I would have loved that chair, but I don't regret not paying his wildly over-inflated price.

I walked away swiftly. I wasn't playing a game to push the price down, and I could tell we were never going to reach an agreement. Instead, I explained that it didn't work for me, I thanked him for his time, and I left.

You will find yourself from time to time experiencing this kind of misalignment of value - where you are not even close to a deal and it is unlikely that you will get there. In this situation you have to **make the tough call and walk away**.

Be very sensitive to cultural nuances when you are travelling. In some cultures, once you start a negotiation, you're in it until the end – and there WILL be a deal at the end. Things can get a bit hairy, so be mindful (and prepared).

☐ *GAVE IT A GO*

Actions for next time
_____
_____
_____
_____

Notes
_____
_____
_____
_____
_____
_____
_____
_____

☐ *GOT IT*

THE LAST WORD

PROFILE   ALL

CLOSE

OVERVIEW

If you've had a great experience, you have the opportunity to share it with others and to reward the person you dealt with.

ACTION

People often take action when they've had a negative experience, but I think it's a wonderful surprise to receive positive praise.

I once learnt that a massive organisation I worked for had a Compliments Department (strange, huh?); a team dedicated to receiving compliments. And I daresay they weren't rushed off their feet. Nonetheless, it was a great experience to receive notification that my team had received a compliment (yep, this was in pre-social media days). Compliments are rare, but they are something people are proud of, so if you're happy why not consider:

- Word of mouth and referrals
- Online ratings and reviews
- Sending a message of thanks

Write a personal email to the person you dealt with, or their boss, to **let them know they did a good job**.

☐ GAVE IT A GO

Actions for next time

CLOSE

Notes

☐ *GOT IT*

Stage 4: It's time to close

for the

masters

For the Masters

Congratulations!

If you have reached mastery by working through this book over time, it's definitely time to pat yourself on the back – the hard work must be really paying off for you now! On the other hand, if you analysed yourself as a master from the beginning of this book, well done to you too! You've put in serious effort to get here.

So, where to next?

Of course, you will forever be practicing and continuing to enjoy engaging in good negotiations. As you do, **please take the time to share your knowledge** and your skills with as many people as possible.

I am disappointed when people don't want to invest in negotiation training for their staff because they "don't want them to use it against them". Honestly! The world is changing and we need to do everything we can to empower our people to feel comfortable handling tricky conversations, to feel like they are being valued, and to feel confident about themselves generally. It's the least we can do for each other.

- [ ] Arrange a ride-along today with one of your team for a situation where you know they will improve their negotiation skills.

- [ ] Work on a problem with your team using Edward De Bono's Six Thinking Hats.

- [ ] Invest in a training program to upskill your team – I know someone who can help you out with that one ;-)

- [ ] _____

- [ ] _____

Enjoy!!

For the Masters

conclusion

Conclusion

Conclusion

Well, that's it. You should now be starting to love negotiating! At the very least, you should no longer feel panicked or uneasy about entering a negotiation.

Whichever profile you identified with at the start of this experience, by participating in the activities, you will have shifted your mindset. You will be starting to see opportunities where you didn't before. And your brain will be more alert to more occasions where you can get what you want – easier than you could have imagined prior to this adventure.

Negotiating is a life skill, and you are now on the road to developing it into a habit. Rumour has it that it takes 21 days to form a habit, but that is just a rumour. I think embedding a new life skill might take a little longer than that, so keep practicing.

There will always be times when you find a particular negotiation challenging, and there are times when it will still feel a bit funky, but that's natural. Remember, you are trying to change a habit of a lifetime.

Over time you will find some negotiations easy, situations where prior to reading this book you wouldn't even have given a go. This will enable you to start tackling more complicated negotiations.

Every time you notice some progress, take a moment to reflect on how far you've come, and give yourself a pat on the back. Continue to push yourself to try new things and congratulate yourself whenever you choose to give it a go. The more you use this skill, the more natural and rewarding it will become.

Back yourself, learn from your experiences and reap the rewards. This is how you learn to love negotiating.

Good luck!

Conclusion

a word of thanks

A word of thanks

A word of thanks

I am so thankful to those who have encouraged me to write this book, but even more thankful to those who taught me these skills. Above all other teachers I think my mum is the one who helped me the most with these skills. When I was an angst teenager she was on the receiving end of what was known in our family as 'the look' – and yes, it got me into a LOT of trouble. I think it was from there that I really HAD to learn how to get out of the trouble 'the look' got me into! Mum has the patience of a saint, and I tested them often and comprehensively. So I learnt about boundaries, early. Thankfully I grew up and grew out of that phase, but not without it shaping the direction of my career. Now I am lucky to have her as a wonderful friend that helps just by listening and loving me – thank you. xo

My next educator is my amazing dad who taught me so much such as how to laugh at the madness, that I really didn't want to go into the Armed Forces (as I wouldn't really cope with people telling me what to do all day) and above all to consider others. He's such a great voice of reason, looking at situations from all angles and helping me understand that this is way to solve problems. Think about what drives people, what they really want from a situation and talk through how to get there, together. I'm so appreciative of your advice and guidance - you're always my go-to person for on the BIG issues and you never, ever disappoint. Thank you. xo

Writing this book came as a bit of a surprise to me as I never really anticipated writing one at all! So thank you to those who knew I could do it before I did – Katie Warner my champion friend and amazing editor, I love working with you and am in awe of your brilliance – I'm so lucky to have you in my life. The incredible Nicky Seaby you have been direct and clear in your feedback, which was painful at times but it made for a better outcome, thank you (and I know the code now). Barbara Barkley, you have been a fantastic supporter, coach, leveller and wine buddy over many, many years – thank you for teaching me grey, it has been an invaluable hue to embrace ☺. And the team at Thought Leaders Business School Pete Cook, Matt Church, Janine Garner and Lynne Cazaly - if it wasn't for your push I wouldn't have got there, thank you!

There are a lot of people I could thank, from all those I have worked with over the years, to all those I have bartered, haggled and tempted to give me a little bit more – thank you!

I love negotiating because of all of you.

About the author

Sam Trattles is a negotiation consultant with 20 years of corporate experience in negotiating multi-million-dollar commercial deals. Her relaxed tone and writing style make it easy to understand complex concepts and to learn how to apply them on a daily basis.

Sam enjoys working with brands, rights holders and individuals to help them secure the best deal, with the best possible returns. She also runs training programs to help individuals and teams negotiate with confidence.

Sam can be reached via either of her websites:

samtrattles.com

othersideofthetable.com.au

CPSIA information can be obtained at www.ICGtesting.com
Printed in the USA
BVOW05s1942121016

4711BVAU00006B/9/P

9 780994 450715